BRIDGES OF CENTRAL PARK

BRIDGES of CENTRAL PARK

by Henry Hope Reed, Robert M. McGee and Esther Mipaas

drawings by Ronald Rife and Joseph LoGuirato

GREENSWARD FOUNDATION, INC.   New York, 1990

This Book Is Dedicated to All the Friends of Central Park.

Published for Greensward Foundation, Inc., by John R. Storb

Cover and text design by Ruth Bornschlegel

Maps by George Colbert

Copy editing by H. L. Davisson

Research by Joseph P. Bresnan, former Executive Director, Landmarks Preservation Commission and Adrienne G. Bresnan, Program Manager for Landmarks, Department of General Services, City of New York.

Greensward Foundation, Inc. extends thanks to Idilio Gracia-Peña, Commissioner of the Department of Records and Information Services, and to Kenneth Cobb, Director, Evelyn Gonzales, Reference Archivist, and photographer Seth Janofsky of the New York City Municipal Archives for their valued assistance in making available the original drawings of Central Park's architects and engineers.

Publication of this book was made possible by generous gifts from

Peter Bienstock
Clementine Z. Estes
Forbes Foundation
The J.M. Kaplan Fund
Lucy and Henry Moses Fund, Inc.
Nelson Olmsted
Arthur Ross Foundation
Mary Cowell Ross
Chauncey Stillman
The Sulzberger Foundation Inc.
Members of the Friends of Central Park

and in memory of

James H. Fleetwood
Estelle Wolf

ORIGINAL BRIDGE NUMBERS

Original bridge numbers refer to the order in which construction began from 1859 to 1875 as recorded in the *Fifth Annual Report of the Board of Commissioners of the Central Park for the Year 1861* and in Annual Reports of subsequent years. The later bridges were not numbered. For this book the bridges are numbered by geographical location, beginning at the south end of the park.

ORIGINAL BRIDGE NUMBERS		AS IDENTIFIED IN THIS BOOK
1	Terrace Bridge *1859–1863*	18
2	Driprock Arch *1860*	11
3	Willowdell Arch *1861*	17
4	Balcony Bridge *1860*	6
5	Bow Bridge *1859–1862*	19
6	Dalehead Arch *1860–1862*	3
7	Denesmouth Arch *1859–1860*	16
8	Glade Arch *1862*	21
9	Marble Arch *1860; destroyed in 1938*	B
10	Bank Rock Bridge *1860*	7
11	Green Gap Arch *1861*	15
12	Trefoil Arch *1862*	20
13	Greyshot Arch *1860*	1
14	Playmates Arch *1861*	12
15	Pine Bank Arch *1861*	2
16	Dipway Arch *1862*	10
17	Winterdale Arch *1860–1861*	9
18	Riftstone Arch *1862*	4
19	Spur Rock Arch *1862; destroyed in 1934*	A
20	Ramble Arch *1863*	8

ORIGINAL BRIDGE NUMBERS		AS IDENTIFIED IN THIS BOOK
21	Gill Bridge[1]	
22	Unnamed[2]	
23	Greywacke Arch *1863*	22
24	Southeast Reservoir Bridge *1865*	23
25	Springbanks Arch *1863*	27
26	Glen Span *1865*	28
27	Reservoir Bridge Southwest *1864*	24
28	Gothic Bridge *1864*	26
29	Huddlestone Arch *1866*	29
30	Cascade Bridge[3]	
31	Unnamed[3]	
32	Loch Bridge[3]	
33	Inscope Arch *ca.1875*	14
34	Outset Arch *1873–1875; destroyed in 1934*	C
35	Gapstow Bridge *1874, 1896*	13

BRIDGES WITHOUT ORIGINAL NUMBERS:

	AS IDENTIFIED IN THIS BOOK
Claremont Arch *ca.1890*	25
Eaglevale Bridge *ca.1890*	5
Mountcliff Arch *ca.1890*	30
Rustic Bridge in Ramble[2]	

[1] Rustic bridge, page 86
[2] Rustic bridge, page 87
[3] Rustic bridge, not illustrated in this book

CONTENTS

RUSTIC BOAT LANDING.   C. Vaux, Arch't.

CENTRAL PARK – THE GRAND VISION

Original presentation sketch, showing intended effect, by Calvert Vaux
From the Greensward plan 1858
Municipal Archives

Were we to glance back over the last century and beyond, one facet of those now distant generations should stand out: the major public works stamped man–made America. Some easily come to mind, the Erie Canal in 1825, the Croton Aqueduct and Reservoirs in 1842, the five railroads linking Chicago and the East by 1854, a list which counts the Panama Canal, Hoover Dam with its Lake Mead, and the St. Lawrence Seaway. And, among them, we can safely place New York's great Central Park.

To underscore its magnitude we can, for one, point to its cost. When finished in 1887, because there were parts unfinished until then, its improvement is estimated at $10,547,451, excluding the cost of the land needed, $7,389,727.96. A comparison of the time is that of the making of the major Paris parks during and after the Second Empire, $8,000,000. Yet another is the cost of the Paris Opera House, one of the last century's great buildings, over $9,000,000.

In mentioning cost we give the park a new dimension. Admittedly, foreigners once complained about Americans, that we were forever boasting in money terms of our monuments. Still, we would like to underscore this aspect of Central Park, that in today's terms, the cost was well over $400,000,000.

And there is imperial precedence for such boasting, that of Caesar Augustus. Toward the end of his triumphant reign the emperor, who was well aware of Man's frail memory, desired to make certain that what he had accomplished would not be forgotten, nor be credited to others. To this end he recorded the *Res Gestae Divi Augusti*, the achievements of the Divine Augustus. It was deposited with the Vestal Virgins and, on his death, copies of it were inscribed on monuments throughout the empire. Not only did he list them, but also what they cost because the money had come from his own ample pocket. (The best surviving inscription is in Ancyra, the present Ankara, the capital of Turkey.)

The park's history is familiar. By 1840 New York had a population of 312,000 concentrated south of 14th Street. What was happening in New York, the explosion of cities, was taking place wherever the Industrial Revolution had touched. England, of course, held out the great examples. The spreading factories which produced the urbanizations were being denounced; already the poet William Blake had written of the "dark Satanic mills." So were the agglomerations themselves, and it became only too obvious that something had to be done to provide the equivalent of the disappearing countryside once found outside cities.

The 1840's heard more than one voice calling for a great urban park for New York. William Cullen Bryant, poet and journalist, spoke out in 1844. At the time there were, in truth, only two recognized public pleasure grounds, the one at the Battery and the other at City Hall called "The Park," both minuscule. A second demand came a few years later from Andrew Jackson Downing, the great landscape architect of the Hudson River Valley. By 1850 such was the interest aroused that the question of the city having a proper park was a campaign issue in the mayoralty election of that year. In 1851 the city's Common Council, on the proposal of Mayor Ambrose C. Kingsland, voted for one. Not until 1853 did the municipality obtain authority from the State Legislature to buy the land for "the Central Park" between Fifth and Eighth Avenues from 59th to 106th Streets. (In 1859 it was extended to 110th Street, and the park attained its present size of 843 acres.)

To take charge of the park's construction a city commission was named in 1854 and almost at once adopted an indifferent park plan. Another three years passed and the State Legislature approved yet another permanent body, the Board of Commissioners of the Central Park, and it was this board which took charge of the site and its improvement.

Of course, the site would be nothing but for the transformation. The driving force for the improvement was the vision of the picturesque or natural landscape, very much part of the cult of nature of the Romantic Era. What is more, in this country, the cult was centered in the Hudson

River Valley. The great pre-Civil War school of painting was the Hudson River School. Nor was it confined to the artist and writer. The above-mentioned Andrew Jackson Downing was the great figure in the landscape art, and not just along the banks of the Hudson. In 1851 Washington called him. He drew plans for the grounds of the United States Capitol, for the Mall north of the Gothic Smithsonian Institution ("the Castle"), and the grounds and parks around the White House. On these last he dealt directly with President Millard Fillmore. If the White House grounds have been much altered, several of the parks which are known collectively as "President's Park" reveal his touch. For example, he gave The Ellipse, to the south of the White House, its basic plan. And he did the same in Lafayette Park to the north of the White House. That he was consulted by President Fillmore gives some notion of his authority. Had he not drowned in a steamboat accident in the Hudson in 1852, he would most certainly have been the planner of Central Park.

Work on clearing the park began in 1857 just as the Bois de Boulogne in Paris was on its way to completion. At this point there appeared the man who would bring about the park as we know it. Calvert Vaux, the architect associate of Downing, was practicing in the city. English-born and English-trained he had, in addition to his professional skills, a considerable knowledge of landscaping both in England and on the continent of Europe. More, he had a not unimportant asset in being able to paint landscapes. He had worked with Downing in 1851 and 1852, and settled permanently in New York City in 1857.

Vaux's reaction on seeing the original plan for the site, adopted by the second commission as well as the first, was one of anger. He promptly canvassed all those of any authority to oppose it and proposed, as an alternative, one selected by competition. The Board of Commissioners went along with his suggestion.

When the competition was announced in October, 1857, he invited Frederick Law Olmsted to join him in preparing a submission. Olmsted, who had been a farmer, nurseryman, writer, editor and even a publisher,

G. Hayward. Lithograph.
D. T. Valentine's Manual of the City of New York for 1859.

VIEW IN CENTRAL PARK.
Promenade. June 1858.

THE PRIME CREATORS OF CENTRAL PARK
STANDING ON WILLOWDELL ARCH

(left to right):

Andrew H. Green, treasurer and controller of the Board of Commissioners of the Central Park.

George E. Waring, Jr. (tentative identification), brilliant engineer who developed the park's complex drainage system.

Calvert Vaux, landscape architect, the man most responsible not only for creating the plan for Central Park but also the designs for the original bridges in the park.

Ignaz A. Pilat, Central Park's first landscape gardener, in charge of all the planting in the park.

Jacob Wrey Mould, associate landscape architect, the chief draftsman of the bridges, who created their decoration and ornament.

Frederick Law Olmsted, superintendent of the park who, with Calvert Vaux, prepared the Greensward plan for Central Park that won first prize in the 1858 competition, and who then was named architect-in-chief.

Photograph by Victor Prevost. 1862. Stuart Collection, The New York Public Library.

had been named superintendent to clear the site. The result was that, when he and Vaux joined, he was in charge of several thousand men and had complete knowledge of the terrain. During the day he was in the park, at night he was working with Vaux. The actual drawing of the plan was done in the latter's house at 136 East 18th Street. On April 28, 1858, "Greensward," their design, was named winner. For the record, Olmsted and Vaux's estimate for their project was $1,500,000.

That New Yorkers accepted the estimate to begin with, as well as the subsequent costs, can be seen in the enthusiasm the park inspired with implementation of the plan. Anthony Trollope, the great English nov-elist who was in this country in 1861 and 1862, recalled it. "But the glory of New York is the Central Park — its glory in the mind of all New Yorkers of the present day," he wrote. "The first question asked of you is whether you have seen the Central Park, and the second is as to what you think of it. It does not do to say that it is fine, grand, beautiful, and miraculous. You must swear . . . that it is more fine, more grand, more beautiful, more miraculous than anything else of the kind anywhere." While he had his reservation of its being an unrivaled wonder, he did say "But the Central Park is a very great fact, and affords a strong additional proof of the sense and energy of the people."

THE TUNNEL AND TRAFFIC ROAD

Tunnel under Vista Rock (The Belvedere) 79th Street transverse. Lithograph.
Ninth Annual Report of the Board of Commissioners of the Central Park, for the Year 1865.
NYC Parks Photo Archive.

It was Olmsted and Vaux's plan, of course, which excited the public and won the recognition of the novelist. He saw the work not long after construction had begun. "At present the Park, to English eyes, seems to be all road," and "the Central Park is good for what it will be, rather than for what it is," were his observations. The key to the designers' success, not just in winning the competition but in gaining public favor, was their innovative solution for the four transverse roads to handle east-west traffic, actually mandated by the Commissioners. They found the answer by sinking the roads and, in this way, taking them out of the park. There were few examples to serve as model prior to their design. One, by the way, is to be found in the sunken streets in the main allée of the park of the Palazzo Reale of Caserta built in imitation of Versailles by Charles III (Bourbon), King of the Two Sicilies. About twenty miles north of Naples it may well have been seen by Olmsted on his European voyage in 1856. If he did notice the Via Camusso beneath the Ponte d'Ercole (Hercules' Bridge) and the Via Tescione near the Fontane di Eolo (Fountain of Aeolus, King of Storms and Winds), there is no record of it in his voluminous papers. Both men actually thought of an example in the zoo in Regent's Park, London.

Whatever the source, the sinking and a tunnel (a tunnel because one had to be carved out of the schist of Vista Rock on the 79th Street transverse), the solution was brilliant. To grasp how brilliant, we need only glance at the failure of the city highway planners of the 1930's and 1940's to follow the Olmsted-Vaux example. A walk in Van Cortlandt Park in the Bronx will make it obvious that much of the Henry Hudson Parkway, as it goes through that magnificent park, could have been given a long tunnel. We might add that the Major Deegan Expressway in the same park could have been given a long tunnel or several tunnels. Yet another sample of the destruction of the same era is found in Cunningham Park in Queens. Admittedly, the answer was not as easy as in Central Park, but the Clearview Expressway could have been so handled that it would not be what it is today, a Chinese wall down the park's center. The Olmsted-Vaux precedent held not the slightest interest to the planning experts of a generation and more ago.

What is most rewarding about the bridges over the transverse roads

C.VAUX, ARCH?. W.H.GRANT, ENGINEER

SARONY, MAJOR & KNAPP, LITH? 449 BROADWAY, N.Y.

ARCHWAY UNDER CARRIAGE DRIVE
FOR TRAFFIC ROAD ACROSS THE PARK

Lithograph.
Third Annual Report, Central Park, for 1859.

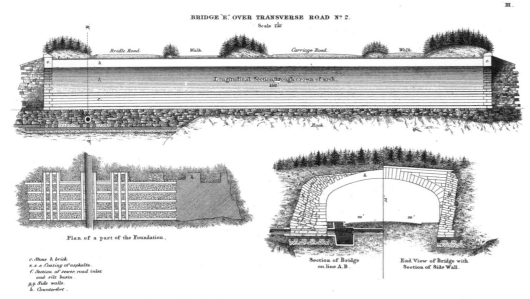

BRIDGE "E." OVER TRANSVERSE ROAD Nº 2.
Scale ⅟₄₀

Bridle Road.   Walk.   Carriage Road.   Walk.

Longitudinal Section through crown of arch.

Rock.

Plan of a part of the Foundation.

c. Stone b. brick.
e. e. e. Coating of asphalte.
f. Section of sewer, road inlet,
    and silt basin.
g. g. Side walls.
h. Counterfort.

Section of Bridge   End View of Bridge with
on line A.B.   Section of Side Wall.

W. B. Swan. del.

Fifth Annual Report, Central Park, for 1861.

SECTIONS OF RETAINING WALLS
OF THE
TRANSVERSE ROADS.

1.

3' 6"

4' 0"

Where the ground declines in rear as a c the
thickness of 8 foot wall is diminished as shown
by rear dotted line

3.

4' 0"

2.

4' 9"

5' 6"

4' 6"

Scale 6 Feet to 1 inch.

Ninth Annual Report,
Central Park, for 1865.
NYC Parks Photo Archive.

is their width, an average of 119 feet. Even the ones carrying only a footpath are wide enough to have space for ample planting to screen the traffic below.

These bridges and the one tunnel are, in a sense, not part of the park, any more than the transverse roads. The bridges which count are those within the park proper. The existence of most of those bridges resulted from a major change in the design shortly after Olmsted and Vaux obtained their commission. True, the Greensward plan had drives and footpaths — few of the latter were indicated in detail—and few park bridges were shown. The change, and it was made at the suggestion of the Commissioners, was the introduction of a bridle path. When President Washington resided in the city, the nation's Capitol in 1789 and 1790, he was accustomed to a daily ride until, for reasons of health, he took to a carriage. With the city's expansion the countryside had long disappeared, and riding for pleasure was limited. With the Commissioners numbering such figures as the banker August Belmont, horseback riding, much as carriage driving, was a necessity. Besides, there were the famous examples of London's Hyde Park with its Rotten Row and the Bois de Boulogne of Paris where fashion dictated a daily cavalcade. This meant that, to the drive and footpath, was added a third right-of-way, the bridle path. The two planners had, from the start, mandated a separation of traffic, easy enough to do with two kinds of right-of-way; now a third was to make for more crossings. In the days before the traffic light a bridge was the only answer.

Originally, there were plans for seven bridges, two tunnels, a masonry bridge, and a footbridge within the park and over the transverse roads. Several of these were given up, and wood gave way to masonry. Then nineteen bridges were added, including the Arcade beneath the drive at the Terrace on the Lake. By 1872 there were thirty-four in the park. In addition, two were yet to be built, and at a later date three other bridges were added, one over the bridle path at the West 77th Street entrance, a second at West 90th Street, and a third at Frederick Douglass Circle.

What is astonishing is how successfully the bridges were made inconspicuous if not concealed. The one striking exception is, of course,

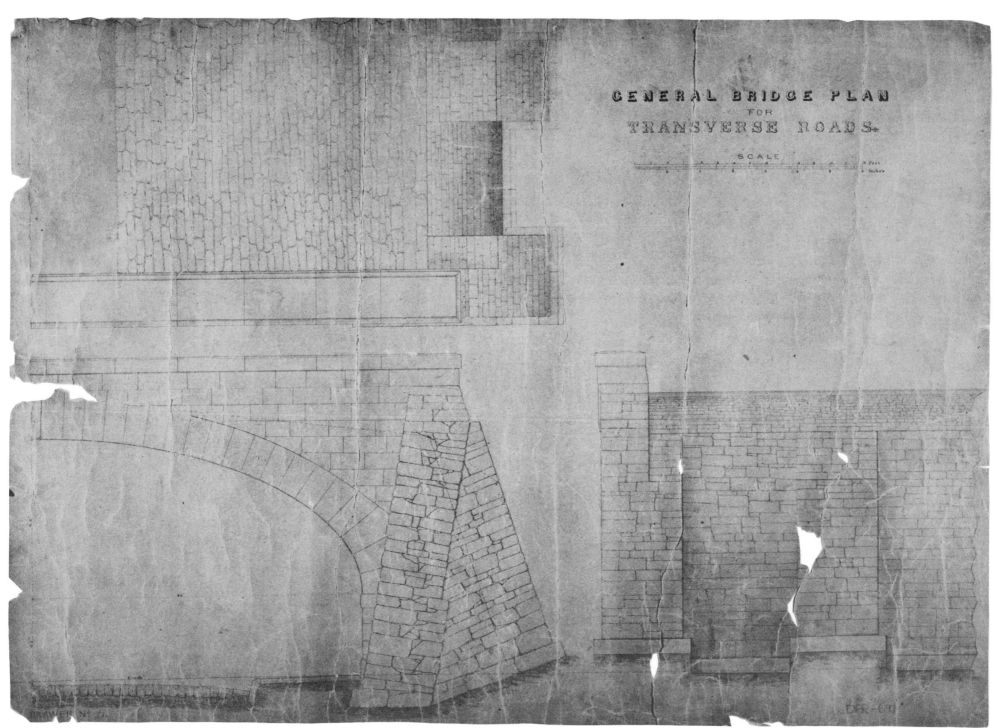

GENERAL BRIDGE PLAN
FOR
TRANSVERSE ROADS.

SCALE

Transverse road bridges. Original section drawing. ca. 1860
Municipal Archives.

Bow Bridge over the Lake. For the others the park visitor, unless he or she is an aficionado, has to pause and think where they are to be found. We tend to neglect them because of the traffic lights. Even more, we remain so taken by the park's overall quality of landscape, the lakes and streams, glades, woodlands, sweep of lawn, that the bridges appear only a minor adjunct, when they are works of art in themselves and in their setting.

Olmsted and Vaux had a very strong conviction that structures had no place in a park, unless they served a park purpose. For example, they were against having a zoo in the park. If the Belvedere Castle was built it was only because Vista Rock, on which it stands, had disappeared behind a screen of greenery, the Ramble. Vista Rock had served as the focal point of the Mall, and the Belvedere took its place with its tower still to be seen above the trees of the Ramble.

Of course, the bridges threatened to be a major intrusion. For that reason not only did the two planners have to site them for convenience, they had to be placed in such a way that they could not be seen until the promenader was at them. A typical one is Willowdell Arch. How many would know that it exists except for the fact that it is near the statue of "Balto," the legendary Alaskan husky? Siting and building the structure was just part of the work; skillful grading—to be sure, almost the whole park was regraded—resulted in concealment.

Hiding the bridges was, in part, a breakaway from the picturesque tradition. In the great English private estates of the 18th century bridges were, along with temples, a conspicuous ornament. Palladio's design for the Rialto Bridge in Venice, never built, was familiar to the landowners as it is found in the Italian architect's *Four Books of Architecture*, and a number of versions of it can be seen in England. In a sense, Olmsted and Vaux had gone a step beyond their predecessors in their vision of a structureless park, actually achieved by Jens Jensen in the Forest Preserve of Cook County, Illinois, in the 1920's.

The designing of the bridges fell to Vaux, and it is testimony to his skill that no two of them are alike. This, too, is part of the picturesque tradition with its accent on constant variety. The materials adopted were familiar to New Yorkers of the time: Philadelphia pressed brick (instead of Hudson River brick); brownstone from the Connecticut Valley; sandstone from New Brunswick;* and schist from the park itself. In order to convey a pronounced rustic note he even used several large uncut blocks of schist from the park. The most spectacular example is the Huddlestone Arch, in the park's north end.

At the other end of the design spectrum are the bridges that are made of cast iron, a favorite of the era, where the architect Jacob Wrey Mould shares honors with Vaux. The parts to be cast would be drawn in exact detail and then sent to the foundry. Large sections, even half an archway, were cast. Cast and wrought iron were innovative. Phosphorous in the iron alloy made fine detail possible in casting. The five remaining bridges in Central Park are outstanding as ornamental iron works in public use. They are also, with the exception of an iron bridge over Dunlap's Creek in Brownsville, Pennsylvania, the oldest cast iron bridges in America.

The bridges of Central Park vary in style, although a Gothic and Romanesque note seems to touch most of them. At the Terrace it would appear to be Romanesque with extraordinary realistic detail. The Gothic is to be seen in a beautiful small bridge of cast iron over the bridle path just north of the Reservoir, Gothic Bridge.

They are a constant reminder that the goal of Olmsted and Vaux was to offer as pleasing a contrast as in their power to the city of brick and stone round about. For that reason they were convinced that nature, without artifacts, was the only answer. Any intrusion, unless serving a park use, detracted from the park's environment, to adopt a modern term. The result is that the New Yorker, let us say with Anthony Trollope's permission, can still boast that Central Park is one of the wonders of its kind.

* The New Brunswick sandstone, also known as Alberta sandstone, was quarried along the coast at Mary's Point in Alberta County, on the west side of Chignecto Bay, an arm of the Bay of Fundy. As the quarries were close to water there was no difficulty in its transportation. The famous tides of the Bay of Fundy evidently presented no obstacle. The stone was carried to New York by sloop and schooner. The quarrymen were Acadians, descendants of early French settlers. The long-abandoned quarries are now part of a provincial bird sanctuary. (From Owen Martin, a Fredericton geologist.)

Outset Arch. Original drawing.
Detail of iron work. 1873
Municipal Archives.

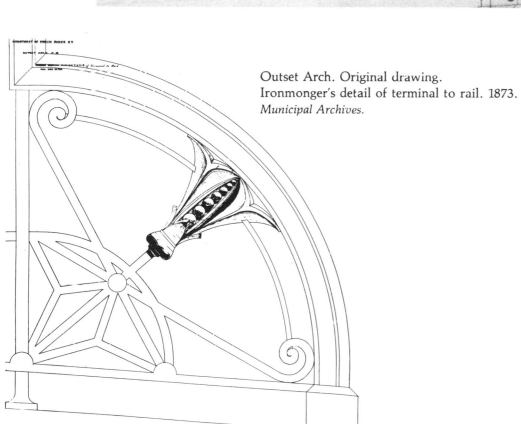

Outset Arch. Original drawing.
Ironmonger's detail of terminal to rail. 1873.
Municipal Archives.

Outset Arch. Original drawing. Ironmonger's detail of rail. 1873.
Municipal Archives.

DRINKING FOUNTAIN FOR HORSES.

ORNAMENTAL BRIDGES AND ARCHWAYS

1. Greyshot Arch

Greyshot Arch is located a short distance from Columbus Circle's "Merchants Gate," just inside the park not far from the Hotel Mayflower on Central Park West between 61st and 62nd Streets.

When work began on the park grounds in the late 1850's, three areas became the focus of construction efforts. Fifth Avenue at 59th Street, the center of the park south of Vista Rock where the Belvedere stands, and the southwest corner at Eighth Avenue and 59th Street.

Carriage roads were laid out with their archways soon after the grading was completed. Most of Greyshot Arch was constructed in 1860. It is like Green Gap Arch, an early design by Calvert Vaux. The arch was in use by 1862, and the 100-foot long sandstone balustrade was set in place a year later. Part of the balustrade is carved with stylized fleur-de-lis. Buttresses flank the archway, rising from curved supports to posts that have round tops in imitation of a modified boss with a diamond point. Modified bosses hold down the supports.

The fountain in Columbus Circle can be seen from the center of the 80-foot wide bridge carrying the park drive. Those sitting on a bench

north of the pedestrian archway on a springtime Sunday will enjoy an unending parade of bikers, joggers and skaters, for this is one of Central Park's most heavily-trafficked areas.

Greyshot Arch is faced with ornamental Westchester County variegated gneiss, a whitish-gray stone with veins of dark orange. It provides a contrast to the muted, earthy New Brunswick sandstone molding of the elliptical arch and balustrading above.

The vaulted archway is lined with Philadelphia red brick and has a 30-foot, 6-inch wide and 10-foot, 1-inch high opening. Greyshot has a passage 80 feet long. Like many of the park's archways, going beneath after a springtime rain takes on the characteristics of a safari through a shallow swamp, as pedestrians without hiking boots tiptoe in reservoirs of mud. Checking erosion of the slopes on the sides of the arch is part of continuing maintenance, much as is removing mud after a storm.

There are nineteen drawings of this Arch in the Municipal Archives. As with many park archways, it should be seen from the walkway on either side to get the full impact of its beauty and design.

Section and elevation of balustrade. Original drawing, signed C. Vaux. 1860. *Municipal Archives.*

2. Pine Bank Arch

Pine Bank Arch is located just east of the West Drive in line with 62nd Street. Standing within 200 feet of Greyshot Arch, it carries a 16-foot wide pedestrian walkway 11 feet above the bridle path.

The cast-iron span was spared when the south and east lengths of the bridle path were eliminated during the modernization sweep of the 1930's. Two other cast-iron bridges over the bridle path, unfortunately, became the era's casualties. Subsequent neglect of Pine Bank Arch over the years almost accomplished what demolition could do in a day.

Pine Bank Arch was restored in 1984 with the Parks Department's plan for rehabilitation of park structures. Steel in the reinforced concrete deck had suffered from extensive rust in some places, and sections of the handrails and posts were missing. Some small cast-iron details had even rusted away.

In the restoration several costly and painstaking steps were involved: the fabrication of missing parts, assembly, scraping old paint and rust on the remaining structure, reassembling and finally repainting. The deck of concrete was replaced with the wood we see today.

Long called Pine Bank Arch, this pedestrian crossover is more accurately a bridge. The 80-foot long walkway is situated between two long, sloping natural rock outcroppings and has two shaped concrete on the remaining structure, reassembling and finally repainting. The deck of concrete was replaced with the wood we see today.

The delicate, ornate, somewhat Gothic handrail was cast in parts and assembled with nuts and bolts. Some of the original drawings bear the signature of the New York Foundry. Large castings were the work of craftsmen from the J.B. and W.W. Cornell Ironworks. Posts and railings at each end of the bridge were taken into storage at the city's facility for monumental artifacts housed on Randall's Island. The restoration allows the cast-iron latticework to be seen again in its full splendor in Central Park. A final touch was planting white pine on the east flank.

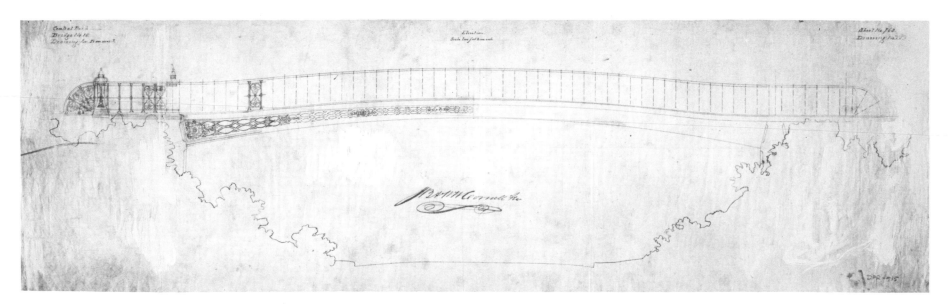

Original drawing for ironwork. 1860.
Municipal Archives.

3. Dalehead Arch

Dalehead Arch is located just inside the Park near Central Park West at 64th Street, a short distance south of the Tavern-on-the-Green. It carries the West Drive over the bridle path with a span 80 feet long. It is 11 feet high and 24 feet deep.

Begun in 1860, like so many of the bridges and archways in this area of the Park first prepared for public use, Dalehead was completed by the year 1862.

The elevations are built of sandstone blocks of random size. The smooth, elliptical arch is hemmed with a brownstone ring molding. Buttresses at the sides of the arch swing out as revetments against the soil embankments that unite the archway with the landscape. Carving enriches the spandrels of the revetments and their terminals. Above, the 77-foot balustrades along the Drive are of sandstone, ornamentally carved with quatrefoil cutouts. The Drive includes sidewalks for pedestrians.

The bridle path passes underneath the archway, and a small open field just outside the western portal is sometimes used by youngsters for softball. Central Park West is within sight, and traffic sounds are omnipresent. At the time of writing, this stretch of the bridle path was closed. One hopes that it may soon be reopened.

Lithograph.
Third Annual Report, Central Park, for 1859.

C. Vaux, Arch.t E. C. Miller, Ass.t   Lith. by Geo. Hayward, 171 Pearl St.

4. *Riftstone Arch*

This unobtrusive archway is near Central Park West and 72nd Street, just inside the park entrance and directly across the street from the famous Dakota apartments. Under Riftstone is the north-south bridle path, hidden from pedestrian and automobile traffic inside and outside the park by plantings. Surrounding terrain obscures Riftstone's elevations and puts it almost totally out of sight; gently-sloping hillsides and vistas in the park draw attention elsewhere. All automobile traffic entering or leaving the park at 72nd Street passes over Riftstone Arch.

By the use of little or no mortar and of megalithic blocks of Manhattan schist the rustic note is conveyed. Vaux's aim was to have some "natural" bridges in his picturesque landscape. Those of brick and mortar would, in a number of instances, have appeared "unnatural."

The segmental arch is low and wide, measuring 30 feet across and 11 feet 10 inches in height. Abutments are concealed in the surrounding landscape by large boulders and surrounding trees and shrubs.

Bearing sharp right at the West 72nd Street entrance, descending to the bridle path past an osage orange, the park explorer will obtain a clear view of the bridge. No one can fail to be impressed by the skillful use of the rough blocks of Manhattan schist from the park itself.

The bridle path has been fenced off to the north of the bridge with no riding permitted south of that point. The problem here, and elsewhere when the bridle path goes beneath a bridge, is flooding. Until the drainage is improved, water and mud from erosion flow beneath Riftstone with every storm.

Horseback riders entering Riftstone Arch, with the Dakota in background.
Bridle Path. Edward Hopper.
Oil on canvas. 1939.
San Francisco Museum of Modern Art.

5. Eaglevale Bridge

This bridge, named Eaglevale for this book, is near the bust of Alexander von Humboldt, the great German naturalist and explorer of South America, at the Naturalist's Gate, the 77th Street entrance on Central Park West. (The bust, by Gustav Blaeser, given to the park by the city's German community in 1869, first stood in the Ramble at the foot of the Gill, then migrated to the East Drive and 59th Street before coming to rest here in 1982.) The bridge was constructed near the turn of the century with the development along Central Park West.

Eaglevale Bridge carries an access road to the West Drive from Central Park West over the bridle path and what was a narrow arm of the Lake going from Balcony Bridge to the Ladies' Pond directly to the south. The Ladies' Pond, considered a nuisance, was filled in around 1936 and its site given over for the playground that is there today. The one-time presence of the Ladies' Pond explains the need for a second arch in addition to the one over the bridle path. That there was once a branch of the Lake here is the reason why the nearby lawn and the bridle path are under water after a storm.

The handsome structure has revetment in blocks of gneiss in rockface random ashlar although the stones are not as big nor as "rustic" as those of Riftstone Arch four hundred yards to the south. Between the two spans, on either side, are balconies resting on buttresses.

Eaglevale Bridge is 150 feet long and 36 feet wide. The west arch is 13 feet 6 inches high over the bridle path and 31 feet wide. The east arch is 18 feet high over the filled-in arm of the lake and 33 feet 6 inches wide.

The few later bridges in the park continued to be built in the Vaux tradition. This was even true of a transverse road. When a new westbound access was made for the 65th Street Transverse on its Fifth Avenue end, it was given a traditional bridge of stone in the mid-1950's.

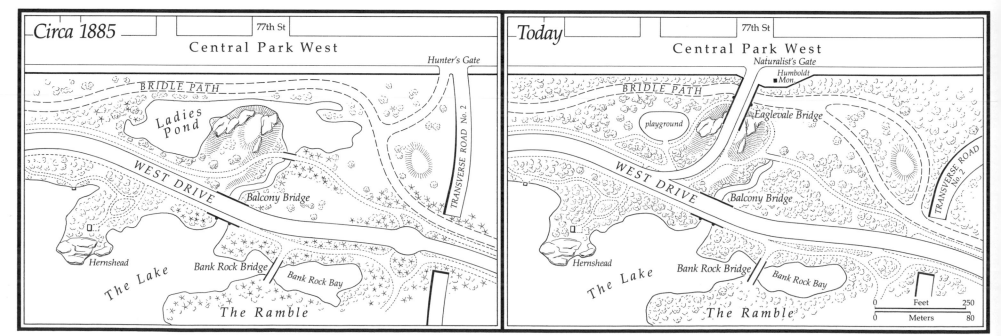

George Colbert, cartographer. 1989.

6. Balcony Bridge

*B*alcony Bridge has a 12-foot wide, 65-foot long walk on its east side. Two bays are corbeled out, forming small balconies with stone benches. With Olmsted and Vaux's plans for a special "winter drive" along this portion of the West Drive, considerable effort went into making this splendid vantage point to view the scenery either while driving, riding, or walking. The bridge provides the most scenic of all views over the Lake toward the Central Park South and Fifth Avenue skylines.

Looking southeast the beholder sees a sheet of water, then clustered trees and, above, the uptown towers of Manhattan. The towers may not have been on Olmsted's and Vaux's agenda but they add quiet drama to the scene. The stately bridge is also located not far from one of New York's great museums, the American Museum of Natural History, somewhat north of the latitude of the Naturalist's Gate.

Eighteen drawings of the Balcony Bridge survive in the Municipal Archives. One sheet, marked as a stonecutter's working drawing, shows the individual blocks of stone drawn to shape with specific dimensions. Calvert Vaux designed the bridge while William H. Grant, supervising engineer, reviewed it for structural values.

Supporting the West Drive, this structure spans a narrow strait between the Lake and what was the Ladies Pond, the western arm of the Lake close to Central Park West. Reserved exclusively for ladies ice-skating in the 1870's, it was filled in during the 1930's.

The bridge's arch is constructed of Manhattan schist excavated in the park, and mountain greywacke, a light-bluish sandstone set in random ashlar. The elevation shows an elliptical arch outline with a sandstone molding and coping. This arch measures 27 feet across and 11 feet 6 inches high, a little more than enough to allow passage underneath while standing up in a rowboat. The underpass is 65 feet long. There are no balconies on the bridge's west side, a rare example of a bridge with different sides, the only other in the park being Trefoil Arch.

Parts of the sandstone railing with open quatrefoil pattern have been replaced by indifferent cast stone rather than cut stone. Viewed from the Ramble, the light-colored stone Balcony Bridge stands out from the lakeshore and is often dramatically reflected in the surface of the water. Its elliptical arch is further emphasized by the jutting prominence of the balcony supports. Clarence Cook in his *Description of the New York Central Park* (1869) believed this to be one of the handsomest bridges.

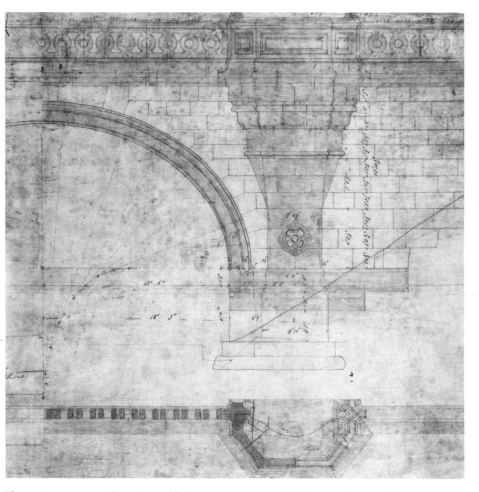

Elevation, plan and section of bridge, parapet and balcony. Original drawing. 1858. *Municipal Archives.*

7. Bank Rock Bridge

*B*ank Rock is a footbridge crossing a narrow arm of the Lake, Bank Rock Bay, west of the Ramble on the latitude of 77th Street. It stands only about 50 yards north and slightly to the east of Balcony Bridge. Originally known as Oak Bridge, featuring the milled woodwork of white oak, the 1860 structure had open cast-iron panels screwed under the railings and between posts. Floorboards were of yellow pine.

Today, it is a nondescript bridge supported by the very same stone abutments and oak trestles placed two abreast and 56 feet apart. The 16-foot wide deck carries pedestrians for 60 feet at a height of only 6 feet and 5 inches above the water.

Sad to say, only three drawings of the original Oak Bridge remain. A mason's drawing shows stone abutments and piers. A scribbled note says: "Thickness of wall calculated for good ground only." A carpenter's working drawing shows the fine detail of fencing along the balustrade.

Since wood construction needs more maintenance than stone, Bank Rock has periodically gone into decay. The present restoration, instead of the original cast-iron railing, has railing of steel pipe.

In 1982, Bank Rock Bridge was rehabilitated for strictly utilitarian purposes. Deteriorating dangerous wood decking was replaced. All the woodwork was thoroughly treated with a preservative; modern steel railings were refitted and painted a dark brown color.

Bank Rock could be rebuilt exactly like the original Oak Bridge, using the same materials in a similar design.

It should be mentioned that Bank Rock is a popular rendezvous for bird watchers bent on exploring the Ramble in spring and fall. Being on the Lake it offers a handy lookout for waterfowl.

Lithograph.
Third Annual Report, Central Park, for 1859.

BRIDGE
FOR FOOTPATH WEST OF THE RAMBLE.

8. *Ramble Arch*

On the west side of the Ramble, hidden in the dense verdure of trees and shrubbery, the Ramble Arch carries a narrow walkway above with an intersecting footpath below.

In calculated contrast to the balance and restraint of the stone archways under the carriage drives, this rough stone structure would seem to have been inspired by some neo-classic landscape in which people dance about in the ruins of antiquity overgrown with vines and grasses.

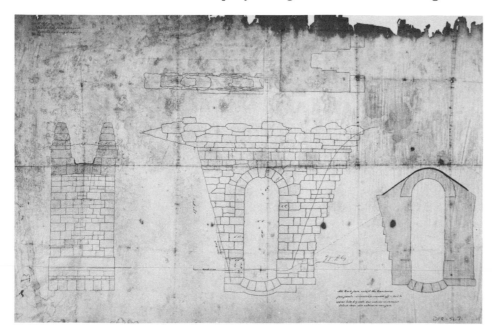

Original mason's working drawing. 1859.
Municipal Archives.

Among the uneven hillocks and trees shading the sun is this narrow structure placed in a cleft between two high rock outcrops. Its arched opening measures only 5 feet across, rising to a height of 13 feet 6 inches. Ramble Arch has a passage 9 feet long and 32-foot sidewalls along the top. An original construction drawing now in the Municipal Archives (shown left) instructed masons to "Select stone with natural or worn face." Except for the base course, the voussoirs and blocks are boulders found in the park, flattened at their sides and "Laid to appear like dry wall, but interior in cement." The rock-face ashlar, which gives it an especially picturesque quality, varies in low relief to being almost flat. In contrast, the parapet walls on top are in pronounced rock-face.

Large boulders specially moved here heighten the dramatic setting. It is impossible to pass underneath Ramble Arch without feeling that you are in one of those very special, faraway places in Central Park.

Just southeast of the bridge's east flank was once an entrance to the Cave, one of the park's curiosities in its early days. The entrance was later blocked. To see the remains of the Cave, the curious have to go to a silted inlet on the Lake side.

View of the Entrance of the Cave and the Arch. G. W. Fasel. Lithograph. 1862.

9. *Winterdale Arch*

Winterdale Arch, along the West Drive by 82nd Street, was so named because it was part of what was known as the Winter Drive. On both sides in this stretch were planted evergreens for winter color. The imposing breadth of its arched opening is enough to host both the bridle path and a pedestrian path separated by an ordinary pipe rail fence running under the dark hollow.

Foundations for Winterdale Arch were laid in 1860, and most of the work was completed, and the structure pressed into service, within a year's time. The cast-iron railings, small portions of the wing walls, and detail work were finished in 1862. Twenty-seven original drawings of it are preserved at the Municipal Archives.

The wide, elliptical arch has a span of 45 feet 6 inches, the largest span of all the stone and brick bridges, and a height of only 12 feet 3 inches. The arch is faced with smooth Maine granite and set in regular ashlar sandstone moldings that follow its contours. Buttresses to either side of the arch curve down to low supporting walls with posts treated as stylized urns. The interior vault and walls are lined with Philadelphia pressed brick interspersed with Milwaukee white brick in a cross pattern.

The ornamental cast-iron railings have been virtually destroyed by repeated automobile accidents. Expedient pipe rail and chain-link fencing have been installed for public safety.

At the time of publication Winterdale is in sorry shape with fallen coping. In its restoration an attempt might be made to bring back the original ironwork.

ARCHWAY UNDER DRIVE FOR BRIDLE-ROAD AND WALK, NORTH-WEST OF THE RAMBLE

Lithograph.
Seventh Annual Report, Central Park, for 1863.

10. *Dipway Arch*

*D*ipway Arch is an ornamental structure underneath the Park Drive near the Seventh Avenue Artisan's Gate entrance to the park. It is near the imaginary intersection of 60th Street and Seventh Avenue. The footpath underneath the archway leads around the Heckscher Playground and north toward the Carousel.

Dipway Arch is one of the underpasses pedestrians use to avoid crossing the Park Drive. From here, visitors used to walk a short distance further uptown and pass over the bridle path on Spur Rock Arch. That span was demolished when the bridle path was terminated on the longitude of Seventh Avenue, and the playground was expanded.

Dipway represents another Calvert Vaux archway designed with a variety of stone textures. Ten original drawings of Dipway remain. The elevation shows granite masonry (the granite is from Rackcliff Island, near Seal Harbor, Maine) set in even courses of ashlar alternating with bush-hammered blocks. The bluish-granite is worked into a dramatically-shaped coping that caps the tops of the archway and curves along the abutments. The segmental arch is small, measuring 15 feet 6 inches wide and 11 feet 7 inches high.

The red brick that lines the underpass is set in stripes of bricks on an angle. The walls are paneled in blind arcades of seven arches, each with a granite keystone. The center bay of the west arcade has been filled with cement. Benches built along the walls invited visitors to rest in the shade. It was another time when archway underpasses provided for comfortable rest and shelter from the hot summer sun or rain.

Fortunately, Dipway's straightforward cast-iron railings have survived, despite their exposed position on the Drive, even though cars have struck them from time to time.

In comparison to other park bridges, Dipway's stonework is in good condition. The excellent quality of the granite, a hard, consolidated, dense rock, has withstood weather and moisture absorption, and has proven to be the most durable stone building material used in the park.

Erosion on both sides of the archway has contributed to a generally shoddy, muddy passage for the pedestrian. This condition often continues for several days after a heavy rain.

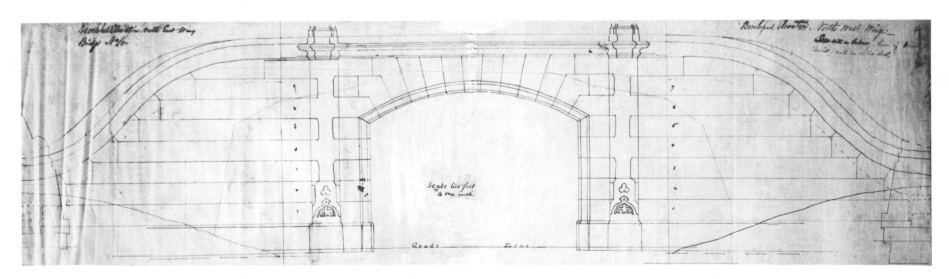

Elevation of northeast and northwest wings. Original drawing. 1860.
Municipal Archives.

R Rije

11. *Driprock Arch*

*D*riprock Arch, listed as fully completed in the *Third Annual Report* dated January 1860, is located under the Center Drive north of Sixth Avenue between the latitudes of 62nd and 63rd Streets. Originally, the archway provided passage for the bridle path later eliminated with the expansion of the Heckscher Playground in the 1930's.

The bridle path extended eastward, passed under Driprock Arch, around the rim of the north arm of the Pond, now filled by the Wollman Skating Rink, passed under Green Gap Arch at the latitude of 64th Street under the East Drive, and turned southward leading to the Scholar's Gate at Fifth Avenue and 60th Street.

The Drive is still carried over the arch but a pedestrian walkway is now underneath. An elliptical archway framed in sandstone, Driprock spans 24 feet, reaching a height of 11 feet. The underpass runs for 65 feet while the balustrade extends 79 feet 8 inches.

Driprock suffered considerable deterioration through the years due to weathering. It is one of the few archways where red brick is used for revetment, combined with sandstone trim at the arch and the balustrade. Octagonal insets with rosettes add touches of color and texture.

Above the arch and red-brick spandrels rests the cornice and the balustrade with its open stone-work of Gothic detail in New Brunswick sandstone. A number of the sandstone balustrade pieces have been replaced by cast stone, an expedient remedy considering the plague of the balustrades along the park drives: careening cars.

Driprock's horizontal line blends with the surrounding landscape. Near its northeastern side is a large osage orange. In the 1850's it was considered very much of an exotic, a native of the Southwest.

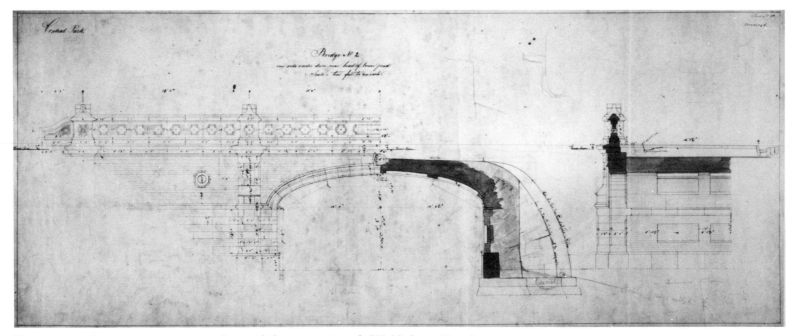

Elevations and transverse sections. Original drawing, signed CV (Calvert Vaux). 1858.
Municipal Archives.

Playmates Arch is a stone and brick masonry structure located just south of the 65th Street transverse. It was designed by Calvert Vaux, detailed by Jacob Wrey Mould and completed by 1863. It continues a pedestrian walkway between the Dairy and the Carousel and also serves as a bridge for the Center Drive.

Lithograph.
Eighth Annual Report, Central Park, for 1864.

ARCHWAY FOR THE FOOT PATH UNDER DRIVE EAST OF THE PLAY GROUND.

Playmates Arch is one of the most ornate masonry structures in Central Park with its characteristic Philadelphia pressed brick and Milwaukee yellow brick-belt coursing and granite trim. In his description of Central Park in 1864, Frederick B. Perkins called Playmates the "tricolored archway." The span is 17 feet 8 inches wide, and 9 feet 11 inches high. The underpass is 66 feet long.

The original cast-iron railing only remains on the east side of the drive. The railing on the west side, destroyed in an auto accident, was replaced with a duplicate cast-iron railing in 1989. This was part of the overall restoration of the Arch by the Parks Department, under the supervision of the Central Park Conservancy. Cast-iron railings, readily available in 1863, are now regarded as special, surviving ornaments.

Playmates derived its name partly from its proximity to a number of major park attractions devoted to children: the Dairy, which once served fresh milk and other refreshments, the Kinderberg, a huge rustic shelter replaced in the 1930's by the Chess and Checkers House, a Children's Cottage, with live animals, and the nearby Carousel. The present Carousel is the latest in a line of three earlier machines in Central Park.

Carousel in Central Park. *Appleton's Journal*, August 3, 1872.
The New York Public Library.

13. *Gapstow Bridge*

*B*earing a striking resemblance to the Ponte di San Francesco in San Remo, Italy, Gapstow Bridge is yet another example of traditional architecture in Central Park. The stone span curves gracefully over the narrow neck of the Pond. Facing south, it offers the quintessential view of the city, with the Plaza Hotel and other towers rising behind the backdrop of trees reflected, amidst the ducks, in the waters of the Pond.

Olmsted and Vaux anticipated 125 years ago that Manhattan's buildings would one day rise around the empty lots by the park, but they could in no way envision the extent of the city's vertical ascent. Today, whether reflecting skyscrapers or simply taken on its own merits, the Pond is a very integral part of Central Park.

The northerly view from the bridge is marred by the sight of the Wollman rink which replaced part of the Pond in 1951 with an ice-skating rink and a crescent-shaped brick bunker. Built on a lake-bottom without proper underpinnings, with the result that it repeatedly settled, the rink was replaced by the present one in 1987.

Originally, Gapstow was a wooden bridge supported by the unique feature of a large segmental arch of wood on the north and south sides, both arches springing from ledges on the stone abutments. Along wood walkway of the bridge the railings were of cast iron. Each of the repeated motifs was composed of a half circle topped by a pointed arch, with the spandrel spaces filled by verticals to meet the hand railing. The center section set off by the intersection of the support arch was figured with three cinquefoils.

Gapstow was a unique design using wood and cast-iron trimming, drawn for this commanding site over the Pond, in the picturesque landscape of the Park. It was to last a little more than a score of years. Conjecture has it that wear and tear were simply too much.

The current stone replacement, designed by Howard & Caudwell in 1896, is built of unadorned Manhattan schist. It spans 44 feet of water at its base with a 12-foot high arch, and it has imposing 76-foot long sidewalls extending the full length of the bridge.

Preliminary study for original bridge. Jacob Wrey Mould. Watercolor. January 7, 1874.
Municipal Archives.

BRIDGES
OF
CENTRAL PARK

BY

Henry Hope Reed
Robert McGee
and Esther Mipaas
with drawings by
Ronald Rife
and
Joseph LoGuirato

GREENSWARD FOUNDATION, INC.
New York, 1989

LIST OF BRIDGES AND ARCHES

14. *Inscope Arch*

*I*nscope Arch was built in response to a traffic problem. The bottleneck of pedestrians that irritated horseback riders and carriage drivers was enough to convince the Department of Public Parks to seek a remedy in the 1870's. At the time Olmsted, no longer officially connected with Central Park, was a partner in Olmsted and Vaux, Landscape Architects. The firm recommended three new bridges: original Gapstow Bridge, Outset Arch, over the bridle path, and Inscope Arch, the only original one of the three that still remains.

Inscope is well worth a special visit. Beautiful ornamental pink granite surrounds the gray granite that borders the half-oval opening of the archway, 13 feet 7 inches across at the base and 12 feet high in the middle. The archway is Tuscan, that is to say, the top of the voussoirs makes an ogival pattern and the bottom a round one. Encompassing the whole above is a cornice in a segmental arc. Inscope's underpass is 34 feet in length. It has a 100-foot-long railing on top.

It was not easy to construct. Olmsted estimated the cost at $50,000, considerably higher than similar construction during the Civil War days. The site was once a swamp. Although water had been drained off to form the Pond, quicksand lay below. Piles were required, and a subflooring of timber was needed to strengthen the rubble schist foundation. It supported a common-brick barrel vault, originally lined with wood sheathing.

Under the 1973 Central Park Master Plan for restoration of the southeast area of the park, masonry pointing, stone cleaning, painting the brick-vault archway a reflective white, and repair of lights inside the archway were completed. Restoring the wood sheathing to the brick-lined walls was deemed too impractical in view of prevalent vandalism.

Inscope Arch is important because it illustrates the continuing creativity of Vaux even after all the designs of the 1850's and 1860's. It is one of those unexpected pleasures discovered when turning a corner in Central Park, nestled unobtrusively in the landscape. Its facings are shielded by embankments, muffling echoes of prevailing urban sound.

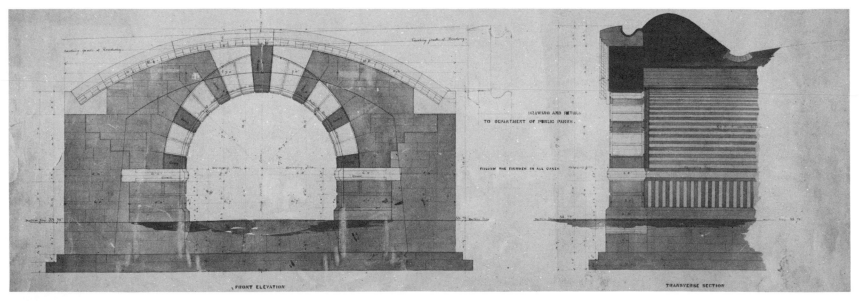

Details of granite and brickwork. Original drawing. 1873.
Municipal Archives.

15. *Green Gap Arch*

Along the Drive not far from the entrance at the equestrian statue of General Sherman, a little over 100 feet of stone balustrading in comparatively undamaged condition identifies the Green Gap Arch below. A walkway under the Drive comes from the Zoo and goes west. Originally it was part of the bridle path under the arch, permitting entry and exit at the Scholar's Gate, Fifth Avenue and 60th Street.

With an underpass 81-feet long, it has a shallow segmental span, 25 feet wide and 13 feet 3 inches high. The facing of Alberta sandstone, from the quarry in New Brunswick, is set in ashlar that continues the outlines of the voussoirs. Posts of the parapet continue downward as supporting piers of the abutments which have, in part, been concealed by the soil of the planted slopes. For the stonework of this archway, Jacob Wrey Mould, assisting Calvert Vaux, made drawings of the details that were then sent to the contracting stoneyards to be cut and shaped to specification. These drawings are in the Municipal Archives.

The attention to detail is seen in the ashlar of sandstone. In addition to being rusticated, the voussoirs are alternately smooth and roughly bush-hammered. The sidewalls are part balustrade and part parapet wall with posts, at the piers, topped by bosses.

The report of the Treasurer of the Board of Commissioners of the Central Park, published in 1861, listing disbursements made the preceding year, names Stewart & Howell as contractors.

Green Gap Arch is another of the large drive-carrying arches, originally serving the bridle path to find its way to Scholar's Gate. The balustrades adjacent to the heavily trafficked drive suffered some deterioration over time, but the original stonework is substantially intact. The severe decay once evident in the soft, highly permeable sandstone was repaired in 1988 when the bridge was made part of the Central Park Zoo. With the Zoo's reconstruction, Green Gap Arch now serves as the westerly entrance from within the park.

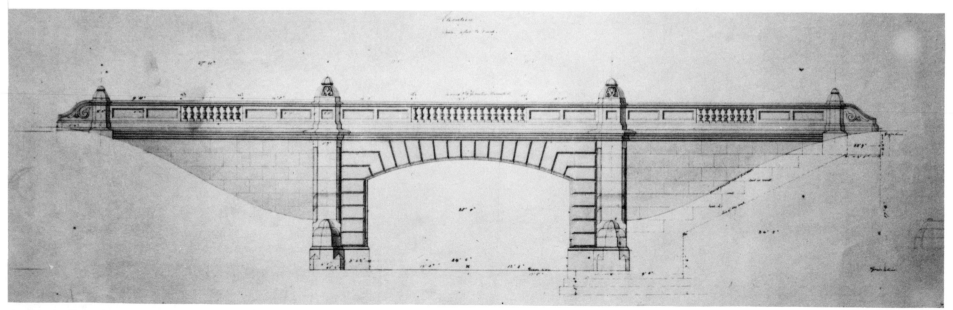

Original ink and watercolor drawing. 1859.
Municipal Archives.

16. *Denesmouth Arch*

Denesmouth Arch, among the earliest of Calvert Vaux's bridges, supports the 65th Street Transverse near Fifth Avenue and permits major north-south pedestrian traffic to pass under the arch between the Dene and the Central Park Zoo. (A block further north, a parallel archway of modern granite was added in the mid-1950's to allow pedestrians to walk north unimpeded, after another access road was constructed for the separation of alternate crosstown traffic).

Denesmouth is constructed of pale-olive New Brunswick sandstone, blackened by years of exposure. The arch is visually strengthened by the voussoirs, alternately long and short, fanning outward, spanning 37 feet 3 inches, with its top 14 feet above the path.

The balustrade of Denesmouth Arch has four large posts, which originally carried ornate bronze lampposts, elegant and monumental in character. Three of these lampposts were stolen several years ago, and the fourth is now in storage, as a model if future replacements are installed on the bridge.

Frequently in the park bridges there is Gothic detail because Vaux was very much part of the Gothic Revival of the Romantic Era. It is seen in the quatrefoil circles of the balustrading and in the base of the buttresses. The surface of the sandstone revetment is part tooled and part smooth. Unusual among park bridges, Denesmouth is all of sandstone, including the interior vault and walls.

Early photographic views of the Arsenal and Menagerie show Denesmouth Arch as a prominent and stately structure providing an interesting transition between the formal area around the Arsenal to the tranquil natural outcroppings by the Dene.

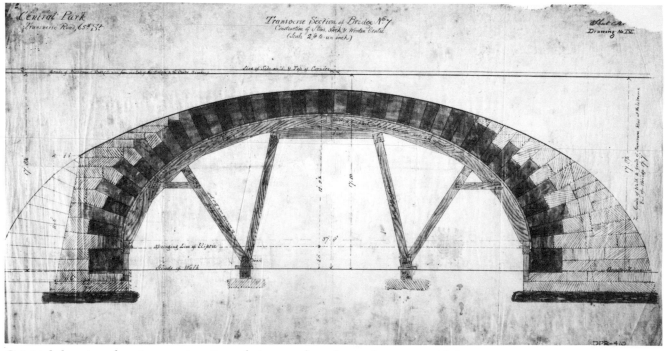

Original drawing showing construction of stone arch and wooden center. 1859.
Municipal Archives.

17. *Willowdell Arch*

Willowdell is a sandstone-and-brick segmental arch located at the East Drive on the latitude of 67th Street between Fifth Avenue and the Mall. Its red-brick facing and sandstone trim give it a resemblance to Driprock, its counterpart at the Center Drive.

There are some striking stylistic details, like the rusticated voussoirs between the abutment and the spring blocks, the coffers of the brick vault, or the keystone and spring blocks, which are vermiculated. The archway has bench seating in the wall arcades. A center niche on the north side once contained a fountain, now broken. The idea was to give mothers a place to rest and relax with their children in tow, though it seems doubtful that the echoes under an archway could give any mother relief from boisterous youngsters for too long.

Above the sandstone coping atop the arch, an original ornamental cast-iron railing has been replaced with more practical wooden parkway guardrails. A treasurer's list of disbursements for 1860 notes a payment to the J.B. and W.W. Cornell Ironworks for the iron railing.

The Parks Department's 1938 survey of bridges reveals an inoperable drinking fountain inside the archway. It also notes an "iron pipe railing in fair condition" instead of the original cast-iron railing.

Willowdell's archway is only 49 feet long, measuring 14 feet 10 inches across and 9 feet 10 inches high. Weathering inside the archway from wind-whipped rain has eroded mortar and created some efflorescence. The park's creators were photographed on this bridge; see page 13.

Outside the eastern portal is a statue dedicated to the dog Balto. It was given to the city to commemorate the efforts of Alaskan sled dogs who transported diptheria serum across Alaska. The monument, dedicated to the lead dog of the last dog team to get through, was designed in 1925·by Frederick G.R. Roth, who was to head the sculpture program of the WPA (Works Progress Administration) in the 1930's.

The inscription commemorating Balto the Dog reads:

> Dedicated to the indomitable spirit of the sled dog that relayed antitoxin six hundred miles over rough ice across treacherous waters through arctic blizzards from Nenana to the relief of stricken Nome in the winter of 1925. Endurance. Fidelity. Intelligence.

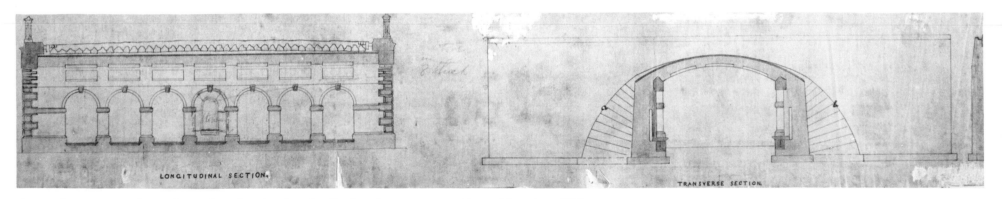

Original stone-cutter's working plan showing longitudinal and transverse section of interior. 1859. *Municipal Archives.*

18. *The Terrace Bridge*

The Terrace and its seven-arch arcade is the climax of the Olmsted-Vaux plan for the park. At the north end of the Mall it faces the Lake and the wooded Ramble beyond. With its splendid site, the careful choice of the designers, it has one of the best, and best known, views in New York.

From an upper terrace, grand stairways on either side descend to an esplanade or "water terrace" below. At its center is the famous Bethesda Fountain. Above the fountain's several basins and irridescent cascade, above its clustered cherubs, stands the Angel of the Waters. Taken together the Bethesda is the city's greatest fountain.

There are several routes to the "water terrace," by the above noted stairways, by paths from the northeast and northwest, the southeast and southwest, but they are all secondary to the main one from the Mall. Here visitors stand at the head of a wide flight of steps announced by two elaborately carved sandstone posts. Descending the steps the curious will find themselves beneath the Terrace Bridge which carries the Drive and the upper terrace. At the foot of the steps is an arcade 29-feet wide and 16-feet high.

After passing through the arcade they are in a columned chamber with walls on either side in blind arcades. In the Municipal Archives are wash drawings for encaustic tile, marble and granite decoration considered for the blind bays in the arcade, but not carried out. The large ceiling was the chief visual element. It was covered with brilliant encaustic tiles made by the Minton Company of Stoke-on-Trent, England. Jacob Wrey Mould who worked with Vaux on the decoration was obviously inspired by Moorish work. It will be recalled that he had worked with Owen Jones on the latter's well-known book on ornament.

Minton tile was once also considered for the floor here, much as it is found today on many floors in the United States Capitol. What is here today are panels of red tile bordered with strips of bluish granite, the whole installed in 1910.

Visitors then leave via the seven-arch arcade to find themselves at the Bethesda Fountain.

Vaux, on his travels outside of England, must have been to the great Palace of Versailles. There he would have seen the famous Orangerie beneath the main terrace. Facing it, the visitor has before him the space where, in the summer, the orange trees are placed, as well as around the gardens. Beyond it is a wall with the round-arch doorways of the Orangerie where the trees are stored in winter. Framing the open space and the arcaded wall are two wide flights of 103 steps, called *les Cent Marches.* In much the same way Vaux has a space, part of the lower terrace with an arcade behind it, and two flights of steps to either side. The park devotee, standing at the fountain and facing south, will be struck by the similarity of the two designs, even if Vaux's variation, both in style and size, places it in a wholly different category.

This structure of New Brunswick sandstone in a typical mixture of styles, Romanesque, Gothic and Classical, seems relatively simple. Our attention is taken by the ornament which was Mould's responsibility.

Vaux's own description conveys the amount of work and extent of care that the park's construction demanded.* It is a sobering reminder that great works of art are not easily, or casually, produced.

---

* The bridge, so far as it serves to carry the carriage road and walk over the entrance from the Mall to the Lake, has a height of 16 feet, a span of 29 feet, and a breadth of roadway of 45 feet. The roadway is supported on wrought iron girders 24 inches in depth, ranged 6 feet 11 1/4 inches apart, and connected with brick arches. The girders rest upon a portion of the main sidewalls of the Terrace structure . . .

The brick arches of the roadway, owing to the mode of construction, admit of but little descent for drainage from the middle to the ends of the bridge, and greater care than usual has been taken to render the work completely impervious to moisture. The brickwork was first plastered over smoothly with cement, a coat of asphalt was then applied, and next a canvas cover was put over the whole, and this again coated with asphalt. This process was extended over the rear of the walls below the freezing point, and the canvas, being well coated on both sides, was then turned outward from the wall and lapped on the sloping edge of a broad puddled clay gutter; in the hollow of this gutter a line of drain tiles, with open joints, was laid, leading securely away from the rear walls; clay, puddled or well rammed, connected the gutter with the original unbroken earth in rear of the walls.

The drain tiles were covered with coarse gravel or rubble, and the earth filled in above to the height of the brick-work and iron girders of the bridge. Additional under-drains receive and carry off the surface water from the bridge and the grounds in the vicinity.

NOTE: Ronald Rife has taken artistic license in turning the Angel of the Waters on Bethesda Fountain to face outward.

Glazed encaustic tile decorative ceiling under
Terrace Bridge.
Seventh Annual Report, Central Park, for 1863.

PANELS TO LARGER SCALE.

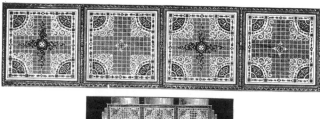

C. VAUX, ARCH.   J. W. ORR, N. Y.

GENERAL PLAN OF TILE CEILING FOR TERRACE CORRIDOR.

Gonfalon at the Terrace
bearing arms of the
City of New York.
*Ninth Annual Report,
Central Park, for 1865.
NYC Parks Photo
Archive.*

Plan of the Terrace.
Seventh Annual Report, Central Park, for 1863.

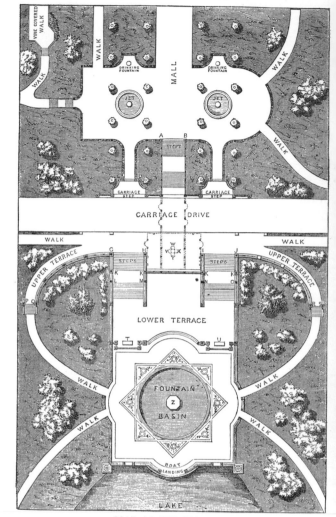

PLAN OF THE TERRACE.

The general terrace structure, of which this bridge forms a part, can only be described adequately by the aid of plans in considerable detail.

About 6,457 cubic yards of masonry of all kinds is contained in the work, including the bridge, and the connected lateral walls extending around and enclosing the area on the north side between the main structure and the Lake. The foundations are on rock, except for a small portion of lateral walls. The drainage of the whole site has been thorough, the water being conveyed and discharged through numerous underdrains into the Lake. Hydrants, connected with the supply-pipe of the Park, are placed at convenient points for watering the area and the adjoining grounds; and a four-inch branch water-pipe is laid to the center of the circle, near the Lake, to supply the fountain and basin that are designed to occupy that position.

The masonry of all but the face-work, and the interior brick arches, is composed of the gneiss stone of the Park. The face-work, trimmings, balustrades, etc., are of New Brunswick stone throughout. The steps and platforms of the stairways, and of the wall at the border of the lake, are of granite. The main platforms of the stairways are formed of slabs of granite, the largest of which measure 10 feet 9 inches by 19 feet 7 inches, and weigh about 15 tons each.

The floor under the bridge and arcades is formed of a bed of clean broken stone, covered with a coat of hard, common brick, laid in mortar. The inequalities of the surface of the rock below the floor, that were liable to hold water, were filled with concrete before putting down the bed of stone, and advantage was taken of the principal depressions of the rock surface, to lay a series of underdrains of the foundation. The main underdrains are, in part, large enough to be entered and examined, and are also so arranged as to admit of being flushed out when necessary. Upon the brick pavement, which is left one and a half inches below the final level, it is intended to lay marble encaustic tiles, to complete the floor.

The area covered by bridge and connected arcades is 5,050 square feet; and the open area north of the main work, containing the site of the fountain, and terminating at the Lake, contains 32,090 square feet. The whole area of ground occupied by and enclosed within the entire connected work, is 63,400 square feet, or 1½ acres. (*Fifth Annual Report of the Board of Commissioners of the Central Park,* for the year 1861)

C. Vaux, Arch: J.W.Mould, Asst:

FOR D.T. VALENTINE'S MANUAL 1864.

CENTRAL PARK.
THE TERRACE.

Lithograph.
Sixth Annual Report, Central Park, for 1862.

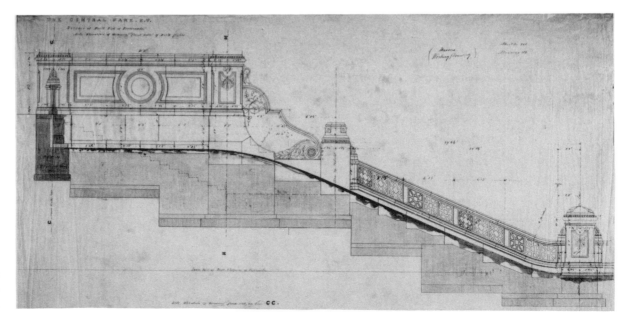

Side elevation of wall and steps.
Original mason's working drawing. 1862.
Municipal Archives.

59

19. Bow Bridge

*B*ow Bridge, so familiar to all friends of the park, stands today as the most revered of all the Central Park bridges. The grace and style of the balustrade and the story of cannon balls set in its base somehow set Bow Bridge apart. Like the others, it is in scale and harmony with the surroundings, connecting the Ramble and Cherry Hill with a graceful arch over 60 feet of the Lake. But Bow Bridge is extraordinary, the quintessence of good design.

Original plans for the abutments' interior note the presence of cannon balls as movable bearings at the Ramble end of the span, to allow the cast iron to expand and contract. Unitized girders span 87 feet, with an expansion differential of 2 to 3 inches from the hottest summer day to the depths of winter's cold. The bridge is 15 feet 8 inches wide and its arch rises 9 feet 6 inches above the level of the Lake. Some 19 drawings survive in the Municipal Archives.

The span was constructed in 1859–60, with ironwork provided by Janes, Kirtland & Co. While work was underway, the company won the contract for the dome of The Capitol in Washington, D.C. Bow Bridge was rushed to completion, with minor changes made to save time. In 1862, the railing was in place.

It was not one of the easier bridges to build. The north bank of the bridge is lower than the south bank, so the northern abutment is taller. But when completed, with its 142-foot balustrade and wood walkway, Bow Bridge became a picturesque backdrop for ice skaters and boaters.

Designed by Calvert Vaux and Jacob Wrey Mould, the interlacing ornamental-iron railing follows the style of the time, piercing with Gothic cinquefoils, mixing details that are essentially classical Greek along with foliated ornament in the more lavish taste of the Renaissance.

Like other cast-iron structures in the park, the bridge, through attrition, would end in disrepair. By the early 1970's, crumbling stone and eroding iron characterized Bow Bridge. Plans to restore the bridge were prepared by William and Geoffrey Platt, architects. In 1974, a $368,000

restoration was completed by P.A. Fiebiger, Inc. made possible by the munificent gifts of Lucy G. Moses and Lila Acheson Wallace. The subsequent structural repair of the original genuine puddle wrought iron plates was funded by The Vincent Astor Foundation and by The J.M. Kaplan Fund.

Vases atop the end posts that were part of the bridge's original ornamental design were not restored. There are no plans to replace them.

Today, Bow Bridge remains one of Central Park's most notable sights.

Terminal of balustrade. 1971.
Ronald Rife.

The eastern side of Trefoil Arch has one of the most distinctive facades of all park archways. A round trefoil, which explains the name, frames the archway entrance in the Gothic style with not one, but two focal points equidistant from the center, a trefoil being an ornament in a three-lobe pattern. The coping has an uncomplicated but beautiful design of richly-carved incisive floral pattern. In the flanking walls are quatrefoils in round frames which, in turn, are bordered by four small circles.

The west side of Trefoil, by contrast, has a round archway. Instead of the floral voussoirs of the east archway, the voussoirs on the west are rusticated and have a curved face. The walls to either side of the archway here have a tooled surface. Also, on the west, there are buttresses that rise to round posts with floral relief.

Perhaps most surprising of all is that the revetment is brownstone throughout. In a generation when brownstone, from the banks of the Passaic and Connecticut Rivers, spread throughout the city and beyond, it was not the favored stone for the park bridges. That distinction Vaux reserved for New Brunswick sandstone. The tunnel inside is lined with common brick under wood sheathing. Cast iron was used for the east railing. Trefoil was completed in 1862 on the designs of Calvert Vaux and Jacob Wrey Mould.

Trefoil is under the East Drive on the path leading from Conservatory Pond to the Lake and Boathouse, in line with 73rd and 74th Streets. Its span is 15 feet 10 inches between abutments, with the highest point 11 feet 9 inches above the path. The underpass is 66 feet and the railing 110 feet long. A statue of Hans Christian Andersen stands nearby. The Board of Commissioners of the Central Park noted a number of similarities between Terrace Bridge and Trefoil Arch in their *Fifth Annual Report* for 1861. Both carry a carriage road and path over another path; both have the roadway above resting on similar wrought-iron girders; both stand on a foundation of rubble stone masonry. The Terrace, a much larger undertaking that connects the Mall and the Bethesda Fountain, represents the grandeur of Central Park. But both structures feature Mould's artistry and provide passages to important vistas.

Trefoil was restored in 1983-85 at a cost of over $300,000.

View of round archway on west facade. Lithograph. *Seventh Annual Report, Central Park, for 1863.*

ARCHWAY UNDER DRIVE FOR FOOT-PATH, EAST OF THE LAKE

Glade Arch, near Fifth Avenue and 79th Street, is among the first of Calvert Vaux's designs. Like Denesmouth, further south, the low elliptical span was constructed with a light-colored New Brunswick sandstone. It measures 29 feet 6 inches across and is 10 feet high. The underpassage is 50 feet 7 inches, and the balustrade extends for 95 feet.

Deterioration took its toll over the years. The stonework lost its subtle tones. Trees budged the structure, coping fell, and the balustrade fractured. In 1980, a snowplow clearing the roadway destroyed a large section of the northern balustrade. In 1981, the bridge was renovated, the stone washed, the coping reset and missing parts of the balustrade replaced. This was made possible by the joint effort of the Central Park Community Fund and Greensward Foundation, with a generous grant from Bankers Trust Company.

Original study for bridge over footpath.
Watercolor and black ink. April 15, 1859.
Municipal Archives

All original stone posts and bases were repaired and reused along with thirty new balusters of reinforced cast stone replicating the originals. Graffiti was removed from the surface of the structure and the interior vault of red Philadelphia brick. Overgrown landscape in the area was cleared to make the restored structure more visible and attractive. In 1988, deteriorated brick in the vault was replaced by the Central Park Conservancy.

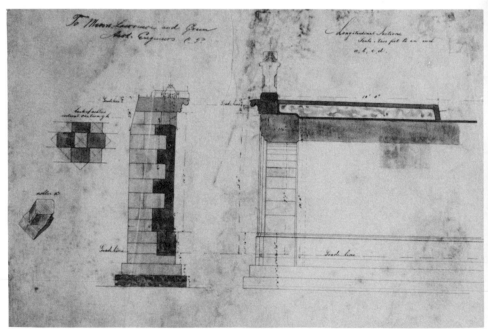

Longitudinal Sections. Original drawing. 1859.
Municipal Archives.

Novel touches are seen in the stonework. The revetment of the abutments is set in a diamond pattern with the surface in tooled ashlar. The device of a sunken quatrefoil is found in each abutment. The rectangular posts of the balustrade are topped by a cluster of horizontal rods.

22. *Greywacke Arch*

Greywacke Arch, just south of the Obelisk, allows pedestrians to reach the Great Lawn by crossing under East Drive via a path beginning at 79th Street and Fifth Avenue, south of the Metropolitan Museum. Construction began in 1861; the Commissioners' *Sixth Annual Report* noted the bridge completed by 1862, except for its distinctive railing. Thirteen of the original drawings remain, all by the hand of Jacob Wrey Mould. The pointed Saracenic arch bears the unmistakable Moorish overtones arising from Mould's work with Owen Jones in drawing the Alhambra in Spain. At the arch's base the footing curves into volutes. Mould's talent, teamed with Vaux, gives Central Park a special dimension distinguishing it among great parks.

Gray sandstone and North River greywacke from the Hudson Valley alternate with brownstone from the banks of the Passaic in New Jersey. The surface of the greywacke is tooled, that of the brownstone bush-hammered. The earthy gray and brown colors form a contrasting, decorative pattern that accents the horseshoe contours of the arch and the brownstone-incised molding above. The pointed ornamental sculpture is featured on both elevations. The iron railing is in an abstract pattern.

The underpass vault is in red brick with white brick inserts. Abutments are fully covered. The span is 11 feet 3 inches high at its apex, and 18 feet 3 inches between abutments, while the passage underneath is 56 feet long. Greywacke was restored in 1983–85.

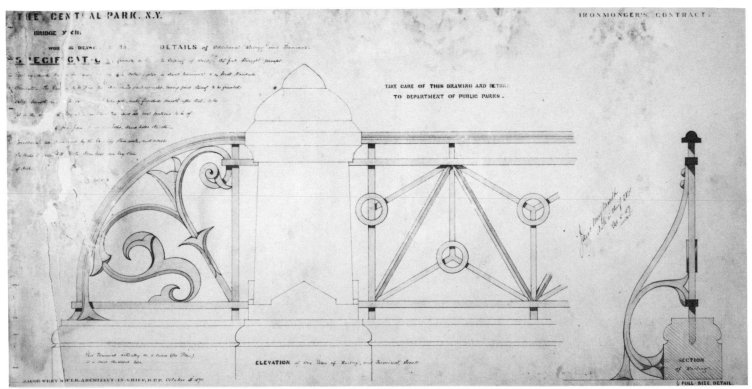

Details from ironmonger's drawing. Elevation showing railing and terminal scroll. Signed Jacob Wrey Mould. October 5, 1871. *Municipal Archives.*

Reached easily from the Fifth Avenue and 85th Street entrance to the park, Southeast Reservoir Bridge is one of three cast-iron spans over the bridle path in the vicinity of the Reservoir. It does not have the same appeal as either of the other two. This could well be because, while the supporting element is suitably curved, the platform above is flat. The bowed elegance of the others is wanting. Nor is there the quantity of ornament and openwork.

It was under contract in 1864 to J.B. and W.W. Cornell Ironworks, which did most of the iron work in the park, and completed a year later.

Much trafficked, it links the Reservoir footpath, a crossing at the drive, and paths coming from two popular park entrances.

The 33-foot long span has a height clearance of 10 feet 3 inches, a moderate size for a cast-iron arch. The span was erected at one-fifth the cost of a stone span, one explanation for the popularity of cast iron in the last century. Fabrication and assembling required fewer workers and less time.

ARCHWAY OVER BRIDLE ROAD NEAR SOUTH GATE HOUSE OF CROTON RESERVOIR.

Lithograph.
Eighth Annual Report, Central Park, for 1864.

Elevation of bridge showing cast-iron railing. Original drawing. 1863.
Municipal Archives.

In 1989, restoration of Southeast Reservoir Bridge was completed by the Parks Department, funded by the Central Park Conservancy. The concrete deck was replaced with a tongue and groove wood deck. New cast-iron railings were fabricated by Historical Arts & Castings of Salt Lake City, Utah, using the original Calvert Vaux drawings.

24. *Reservoir Bridge Southwest*

Reservoir Bridge Southwest, at the southwest corner of the Reservoir, permits visitors to cross over the bridle path without interfering with the equestrians.

The stone abutments, substantially below ground, support the 38-foot 2-inch-wide and 10-foot 9-inch-high arch and a 72-foot span with openwork ornament. The floral scrolls of the cast-iron spandrels and railing reflect an innovative motif of interlacing leaves and curling forms. The posts have tops in the shape of modified urns.

Like the other cast-iron bridges, lack of maintenance and neglect brought about rust, corrosion, and vandalism. In the early 1970's a restoration program, under Director of Historic Parks Joseph Bresnan, combined city and private funds to begin rehabilitation of Central Park's bridges and archways; this bridge was completed in 1979.

Reconstruction of the bridge first necessitated complete removal of all cast iron. Usable railings and ornamentation were salvaged, stripped of encrusted paint, and prepared for reinstallation. The gutter curb and cornice moldings were all numbered for replacement due to the severe deterioration of the original sections. Missing elements were cast from new patterns.

The main structural steel girders were rehabilitated. New structural-steel, cambered "I" beams, were used to support the new wood decking. After reassembly, the entire structure was painted a rich green, a color selected on the basis of a paint-chip analysis of the old structure. It stands today just as Calvert Vaux first saw it built.

The cast-iron bridges in Central Park are the best surviving collection of cast-iron bridges in America. They are important not only because of the beauty of their design, but because of their role, from the point of view of industrial archeology, in the transition of cast iron to steel.

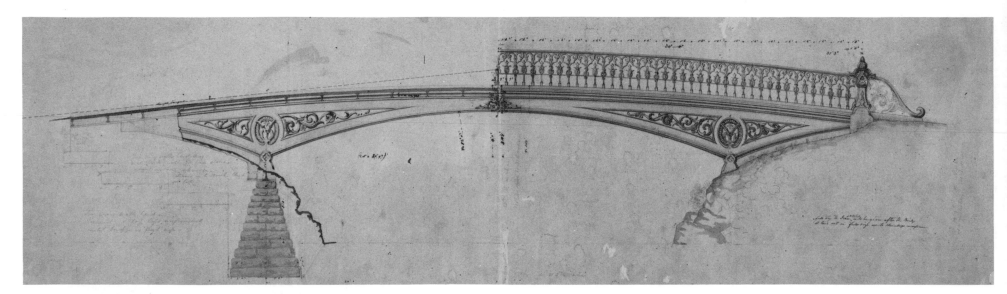

Elevation with detail of cast-iron railing. Original drawing. 1864.
Municipal Archives.

25. *Claremont Arch*

The bridge at Central Park West and 90th Street had no name. As it is over this bridge that the cavaliers enter the park, and as the Claremont Riding Academy at 175 West 89th Street is the only survivor of the many stables once found around the park, it seems appropriate to adopt the Academy's name, which was originally that of a country house that once stood north of Grant's Tomb.

Like Eaglevale Bridge at 77th Street, Claremont is a latecomer, built as part of an access road to the West Drive. It stands just inside the park to the north of the entrance with the Reservoir some 80 yards to the east. Riding enthusiasts have, for more than half a century, appropriated the entrance; it is the most convenient, if not the only entrance, with the bridle path a few feet beyond the Drive at this point.

It should be explained that a few portions of the park were left un-finished for years. One was the northwest side where even the park wall was not completed until the 1880's. Whereas private houses lined Fifth Avenue north of 59th Street, Central Park West was to have large open lots not filled with apartment buildings until a start in the 1880's.

The bridge has an arch approximately 8 feet high, 9 feet 4 inches wide and 58 feet long, the length explained by its being beneath the access road. The stone is Manhattan schist in rockface ashlar. The parapet walls, also of schist, are about forty feet long. The bridge has unusual elevations in that, horizontally, they take the shape of an elongated S. It is not that the anonymous designer took the English painter Hogarth's line of beauty as model, as much as that the access road curves to the Drive. The later bridge builders, following Vaux, simply continued the tradition of having different designs.

Sleighing in Central Park. T. de Thulstrup. *Harper's Weekly*, February 18, 1888.

This famous cast-iron bridge, designed by Calvert Vaux and erected near the north gatehouse of the Reservoir by 94th Street, was long known simply by number. Yet, it seemed somehow deserving of a name and has lately received one, appropriately, "Gothic Bridge."

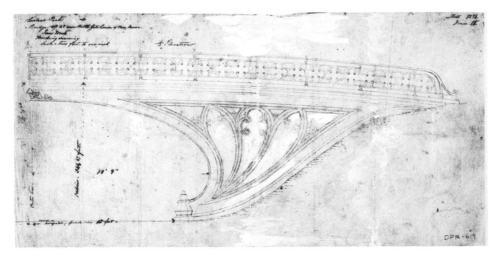

Half elevation. Ironwork. Original working drawing. 1863.

The third of the cast-iron bridges around the Reservoir—like the other two, permits visitors to avoid crossing the bridle path. Equestrian traffic today hardly mandates the presence of the bridge, but it remains as a fanciful addition to the landscape, for the visitor's delight.

The cast-iron spandrels are developed like Gothic windows modified into windblown curves conforming to the oval contours of the arch. Floral crockets adorn the inside of the curves. Graceful and distinctive, the archway is 37 feet 5 inches at its widest point and reaches a height of 15 feet 3 inches. Gothic Bridge is 11 feet 7 inches wide and has a 93-foot railing. It was manufactured by the J.B. & W.W. Cornell Ironworks. The abutments are of Manhattan schist from the park.

Like so many other structures in the park, Gothic Bridge fell into disrepair. Before restoration could begin, successive stages of the 19th century construction process had to be retraced. The careful, skilled work of the old foundrymen had to be examined and duplicated. Today's foundrymen had to check the old cast iron for flaws and repair it by grinding down the separate pieces into new crisp outlines.

Planning began in 1976, based on the nine surviving original drawings now at the Municipal Archives. New drawings were prepared by the Design Division of the Parks Department. Work was underway by 1981 and restoration was completed two years later.

ARCHWAY UNDER FOOT-PATH FOR BRIDLE ROAD, SOUTH OF THE MEADOWS

Lithograph.
Seventh Annual Report, Central Park, for 1863.

27. *Springbanks Arch*

Springbanks Arch, with a striking resemblance to some of the archway facades at Regent's Park in London, is a shaped-stone and brick-masonry structure located at the north flank of the North Meadow on the latitude of 102nd Street. It was designed by Calvert Vaux, detailed by Jacob Wrey Mould in 1862, and completed in the next year.

A short flight of uneven slab steps leads down to its underpass. Its semicircular arch is segmented with rough stone from the Hudson River Valley. Narrow, long, but with little headroom, the archway measures 17 feet 5 inches across, 9 feet 2 inches high and 71 feet long. Red brick lines the passage. A modified entablature follows the shape of the arch at the center and extends outward along the revetments that curve at right angles into the soil. The abutments are covered with soil and planting. A cast-iron railing on the south side is 50 feet 8 inches long.

Springbanks is among the more obscure Central Park archways. It passes under the bridle path and a defunct bit of the Drive once used as a link between the East and West Drives. The concrete walk beneath the arch was originally one half its present width. A stream fed by a spring that drains the North Meadow south of the arch flowed underneath as well, adjacent to the walkway, similar to the passage beneath the Glen Span, but the Springbanks passageway is twenty feet longer.

The spring is now piped beneath the concrete pavement. You may hear water rumbling, but you cannot see it.

In an early spring freshet, with the melting snow and much rain, the flood of water draining from the North Meadow cascades beneath the bridge. Rushing north it joins Montayne's Rivulet to flow underneath the Lasker Rink into the Harlem Meer. The park amateur who ventures here on any day of hard rain will see one of the more astonishing sights in the park, what appears to be a veritable Niagara.

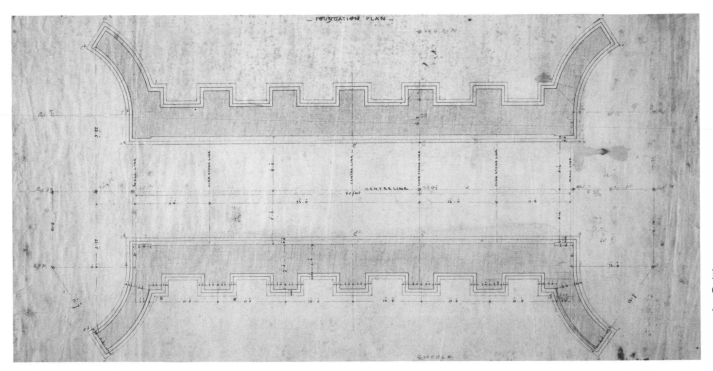

Foundation plan.
Original engineer's drawing. 1863.
Municipal Archives.

28. Glen Span

Glen Span, carrying the West Drive on the latitude of 102nd Street, serves as a gateway to the wooded and secluded Loch to the northeast, surrounded by rustic bridges and what almost seems like a forest. A pathway and a babbling brook run under its archway. To the west is a view of a cascade falling from the Pool on its way toward Harlem Meer. The brook is artificial because the Pool above is fed by city water. The streambed belonged to a preexisting stream known as Montayne's Rivulet.

Like Huddlestone and Springbanks, the other major archways in the Ravine, Glen Span is below the general grade of the surrounding park. These stone structures and several small rustic wooden bridges, including one nearby, just above the cascade, enhance the wilderness setting that Olmsted and Vaux sought to create.

A visit to this deep glen is a pleasant diversion in one of the more isolated areas in the park, a birdwatcher's favorite in the spring.

Lithograph, showing original wooden trestles.
Seventh Annual Report, Central Park, for 1863.

RUSTIC BRIDGE, FOR CARRIAGE DRIVE, NORTH OF THE MEADOWS.

Elevation and transverse section. Original engineer's drawing, showing grottos. 1863.
Municipal Archives.

The arch is built of large-sized, light-gray gneiss, roughly dressed and laid in ashlar. Boulders are piled randomly around the boulder-abutments placed at the time of original construction. Ornamental detail includes a belt course at the spring line, some pentagonally-shaped voussoirs and upright members on each side of the east-arch elevation.

Original drawings show a different Glen Span: rustic wooden trestles, supported by rock piers, with a wooden walk and railing. Designed by Calvert Vaux and Jacob Wrey Mould, it was begun in 1863 and completed with its wooden superstructure two years later. The wood portion was replaced around 1885 with rustic stone. The span width is 16 feet with a height of 18 feet 6 inches. The underpassage is some 50 feet alongside the brook. The sidewalls on top are 65 feet long.

Within the underpass are wide archways to either side. The one to the south by the path is shallow, the north one deep. Purely decorative, these grottos are vestigial remains of a popular device of the Picturesque style.

29. *Huddlestone Arch*

Of all the archways in Central Park, Huddlestone is the most picturesque. To sit at Huddlestone's southern portal on a spring day in the Ravine is not to be in New York, but in a country setting where forsythia abounds and the sound of a gently-flowing brook soothes the spirit.

It is a part of the park that is much more natural, unspoiled, and much less utilized, bordering the Harlem Meer, while providing a less-trafficked retreat off the beaten path. Things change above it, however, since Huddlestone carries the Drive.

The bridge is striking for the immense size of its boulders. One lodged in the base is reputed to weigh close to one hundred tons. Vaux's instructions to the men building Huddlestone were to choose boulders lying around the park that were most reminiscent of untamed nature. Unlike many bridges further south in the park with precisely-cut stone in ordered patterns or with delicate ironwork, the boulders of Huddlestone Bridge look as if they were brought together by some natural phenomenon that just happened to leave a 22-foot wide, 10-foot high arch. But, like all the other park bridges, it also was man-made.

A stream, parallel to the footpath, runs through Huddlestone's archway, disappearing from view at the northern end, when suddenly the natural juxtaposition of trees, rocks, and a brook is ruptured by asphalt, fences, and the concrete mass of the Lasker Rink.

Huddlestone was created in 1866. Almost ninety years later, an ice-skating rink and swimming pool were built north of it when several wealthy sisters decided it would be nice to "do something" for Central Park. Parks Commissioner Newbold Morris, horrified by it, fought the plan to build the massive structure. Unfortunately, he was overruled.

In season, one of the attractions of Huddlestone is the lacelike vines that spill over the cyclopean rock on the bridge's south side.

Recently there have been attempts to deny credit for Huddlestone to Calvert Vaux in the mistaken belief that Olmsted was responsible for massive rustic bridges in the park. In view of the former's instructions to the builders in this instance, it is obvious that the guiding artistic hand, as elsewhere in the park, was that of Vaux.

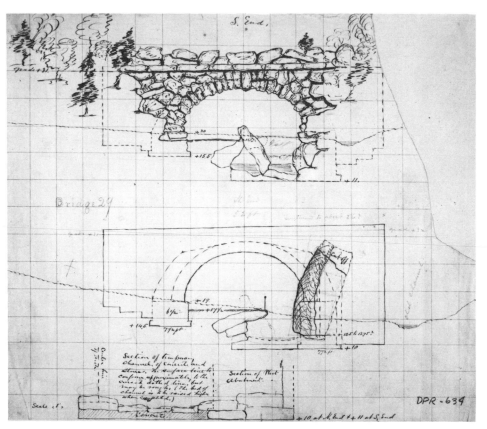

Original sketch. 1866.
Municipal Archives.

30. *Mountcliff Arch*

We have noted that a third wave of bridges came to the upper west side of the park in the 1890's. The newly populated Central Park West called for access to the Drive. The last of the three constructed is Mountcliff Arch, as it has been named for this book, off Frederick Douglass Circle at Central Park West, 110th Street and Cathedral Parkway.

As the other two to the south, Claremont Arch and Eaglevale Bridge, it is built of gneiss in rockface ashlar. Material and handling are suitably rugged for this end of the park, which has its steepest slope along with a nearby cliff. It is a big bridge, being 102 feet long and 48 feet high, with a Tuscan arch some 16 feet high and 21 feet wide.

What is, of course, significant in these massive stone bridges is that they represent a continuing tradition, similar in style to Glen Span.

The park's heritage was not tossed aside as if in anticipation of the revolution in transportation which came with the automobile. Interestingly enough, attractive stone bridges were often part of the parkway designs in the 1930's, which represented, as we now know, a dying tradition.

Overhanging rocks on West Drive near Mountcliff Arch. Joseph LoGuirato. 1989.

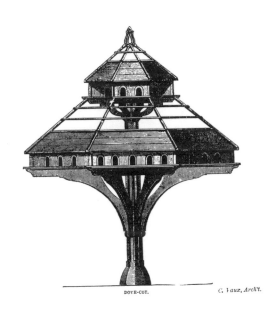

DOVE-COT.   C. Vaux, Arch't.

SMALL RUSTIC BRIDGES and LOST BRIDGES

SMALL RUSTIC BRIDGES

The bridges of Central Park are basically of two classes. The transverse road bridges fall into one category. They were built solely for utility, not intended to be seen or to be conspicuous in the park. Their principal feature in the overall design is that of being screened from observation from the park. The second category, which Olmsted and Vaux called the ornamental bridges or archways, is found along the drives, the bridle paths and foot paths. Each one is of a unique design. The facings of these bridges are of specially selected stone, brick and decorative iron work, as detailed in this book.

There is yet another category, the rustic bridges, those mostly of wood which cross over streams. They were originally built of rough, durable timber in its natural state—red cedar, sassafras and oak. For example, there are two wood bridges on the Gill that flows west through the Ramble. The one at the foot of the stream at the Lake (original bridge number 21, Gill Bridge) has been destroyed as a result of vandalism and rebuilt a good number of times over the years. Only in its latest restoration by the Central Park Conservancy has it been given the railings of contorted branches considered essential in the Romantic era for a bridge in a picturesque park. The Gill's other bridge (which had no original bridge number) is well within the Ramble at the top of the slope to the east. Rebuilt in the 1970's by the carpentry staff of the Parks Department, under the late William Hillman, it does not have the twisted branches of the bridge at the foot of the stream. Here, old wood parkway lampposts were the source of the lumber. The enterprising head of the staff

Gill Bridge. Original bridge No. 21,
Construction date, 1860.
View of the Bridge at the Outlet of the Spring.
G. W. Fasel. Lithograph. 1862.

obtained the well-seasoned wood when the lampposts were being replaced by galvanized steel posts. If the straight timber is hardly picturesque, it is solid and seasoned, with the result that it has lasted almost two decades.

Two similar bridges are to be seen over Montayne's Rivulet in the north end of the park (original bridge number 31, east of Glen Span, which had no name, and original bridge number 32, west of Glen Span, called Loch Bridge.) Again, Department carpenters rebuilt them of wood from the same source. One curiosity nearby is seen in the partly ruined small bridge (original bridge number 30, called Cascade Bridge) over the run-off stream that drains the North Meadow, flowing northerly from beneath Springbanks Arch into Montayne's Rivulet.

Visitors would have found another rustic bridge, in early years, over the western arm of the Lake at the Ladies' Pond (original bridge number 22, shown below). The Pond was filled in for a playground in the mid-1930's. All that remain today of the bridge are planks of wood over a gulley. (See maps on page 30 which show the Ladies Pond, the playground, and the location of the old rustic bridge.)

G. W. Fasel. Lithograph. 1862.

ABOVE AND BELOW: Rustic bridge in Ramble. No original bridge number. Construction date, 1860.

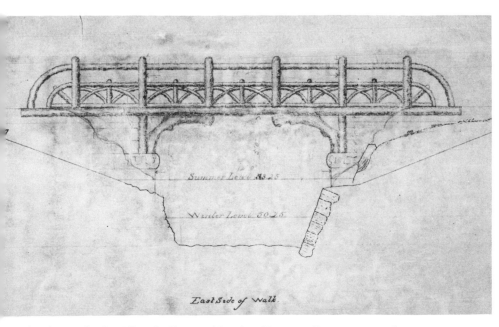

stic bridge at Ladies' Pond. Original bridge No. 22. Construction date, 1861.
ction of bridge, site, and water levels in summer and winter.
iginal drawing. 1860. *Municipal Archives.*

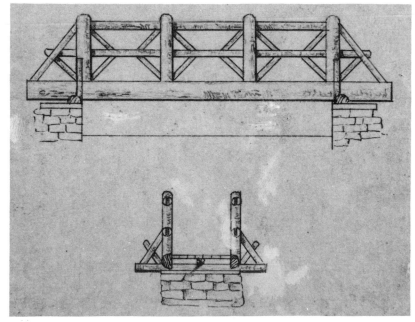

Original drawings. *Municipal Archives.*

LOST BRIDGES

A. *Spur Rock Arch*

ORIGINAL BRIDGE NO. 19
CONSTRUCTION DATE, 1861; DESTROYED, 1934

Spur Rock Arch, sometimes called Oval Arch, was located on the longitude of Seventh Avenue and the latitude of 61st Street. It spanned the bridle path a short distance from Dipway Arch. It was 25 feet long and rose 12-and-a-half feet above the bridal path.

The knuckle of Manhattan schist, against which one of its abutments leaned, gave Spur Rock its name. Both abutments were buried in soil and planted heavily. The distinctive oval outline of its archway and the 'S' curve sides were repeated later with different dimensions for Gothic Bridge. The ornament of the spandrels was altogether different although both designs stemmed from the Gothic, with Spur Rock's spandrels filled and braced by large wheels with interior cusping, not unlike some church windows. The supporting members were wrought iron; the more finely drawn decorative members were cast iron.

Spur Rock was demolished because it got in the way of the expansion of the Heckscher Playground. Instead of being incorporated into the playground, Spur Rock, probably looking old-fashioned, rundown and unimportant in 1934, was destroyed. It was, in fact, irreplaceable. Six drawings of the arch survive at the Municipal Archives.

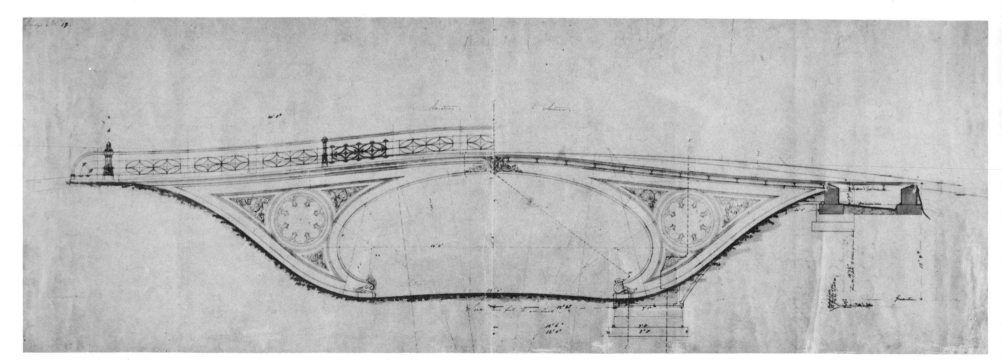

Half elevation and section of bridge, abutment and girder. Original drawing. 1861.
Municipal Archives.

Details of cast-iron posts. Original drawing. 1861.
Municipal Archives.

Lithograph.
Third Annuul Report, Central Park, for 1859.

C. VAUX, ARCHT.   E. C. MILLER, ASST   SARONY, MAJOR & KNAPP, LITH, 449 BROADWAY, N.Y.

ARCHWAY UNDER FOOTPATH
FOR BRIDLE ROAD SOUTH OF PLAYGROUND.

B. *Marble Arch*

The Marble Arch succumbed to the demands of 20th century automobile traffic. It was once located at the latitude of 66th Street, providing a crossing under the Drive, with a stairway up to the southern entrance of the Mall. It was demolished in 1938.

Clarence Cook wrote of this graceful, restful underpass in *A Description of the New York Central Park*, published in 1869:

> This is one of the pleasantest and most elegantly built of all these cool places for rest and refreshment. It is entered at one end of a level with a foot path; at the other a double stairway to the left and right leads to the level of the Mall and to the carriage-road which this archway is designed to carry. It is called the *marble archway* to distinguish it, all other structures of this sort in the Park being built either of stone, or brick, or of brick and stone combined. The marble employed is the coarse limestone from the Westchester quarries. . . . A marble bench runs along each side, and at the end, . . ., a semicircular niche accommodates those who prefer the fuller light that reaches from the stairway. In this niche there is to be placed a suitable marble basin with drinking cups, but, present water is obtained from a common hydrant. The interior of this archway is peculiarly light and attractive, and far more cheerful than other structures of a similar sort in the Park. Here, on a warm day, the children and their nurses gather with their luncheon-baskets, or the reader with his book and sandwich. . . .

Marble is a stone subject to erosion with time. But neglect and new priorities were more to blame—if in fact the archway was in bad condition—when it was demolished.

Marble Arch was found to be obsolete when the plan of the Center Drive and the East Drive was realigned for speedier automobile traffic.

The arch was collapsed and is presumed to still exist beneath the ground. The precise location is known but, to date, no archaeological effort has yet been made to unearth it.

Marble Arch exemplified another functional purpose of the many pedestrian arches in Central Park—that of a shelter. Somewhat similar to Willowdell Arch, Marble Arch had continuous benches on both sides and a drinking fountain. Its freer detail reflected a similarity with the aesthetically complete interiors and ceilings of some bridges and archways, most notable among them the Terrace Bridge.

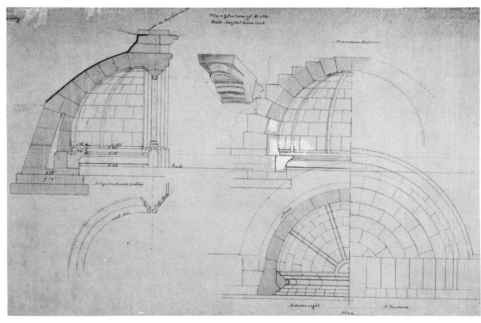

Plan and sections of grotto. Original engineer's drawing. 1861. *Municipal Archives.*

Southwest elevation. Original engineer's drawing. 1861
Municipal Archives

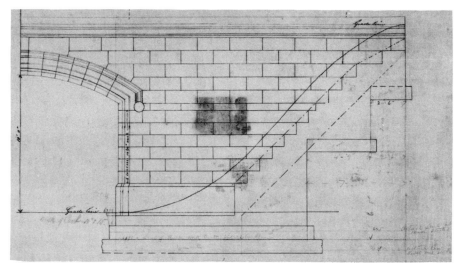

Marble Arch was the only archway built of marble in Central Park. Its demolition was unnecessary. It must be remembered that the 1930's, and for several decades after, was very much an era of tearing down and building anew.

Parks Department policy reflected the era's outlook. In the 1930's, with the ever-increasing number of cars, the drives were straightened in various places. Marble Arch fell victim to fashion. Today, preservation is a force. Were Marble Arch still extant, it would be preserved.

C. VAUX ARCHT   E.C. MILLER . ASST

SARONY. MAJOR & KNAPP. LITH 449 BROADWAY. N.Y.

ARCHWAY UNDER CARRIAGE DRIVE

Lithograph.
Third Annual Report, Central Park, for 1859.

C. Outset Arch

*A*familiar sight in the park in the 1930's, in the neighborhood of 64th Street, was Alfred E. Smith, former Governor of New York State who lived at 820 Fifth Avenue. Dressed all in brown, even to a brown derby, he would be seen going to the Menagerie. The Menagerie, to say the least, was hardly up to animal care standards even for those days. So when Robert Moses was named Park Commissioner by Mayor La Guardia, the former Governor asked his old protegé to do something about the cages and generally poor condition of the animals. The result was the Central Park Zoo.

On deciding to build the Zoo, the Department took more park land: Outset Arch, which was in the way, was destroyed.

Outset was a cast-iron bridge spanning the bridle path at roughly the southwest corner of the present Zoo. Originally, the bridle path came east around the north end of the Pond, then went under Green Gap Arch to turn south and exit at 60th Street. Due to the ever-growing popularity of the park, there resulted a second wave of bridge construction, after the Civil War, chiefly in the south end. Outset was started in 1873 and finished in 1875. Like the still-standing Pinebank Arch, and the vanished Spur Rock Arch, Outset had an elaborate arch, railings and posts as we know from fourteen surviving drawings. The cast-iron tracery and other ornament, very much part of the Civil War Era, distinguished it. Today, of course, were it still standing, it would have been preserved and restored as were Bow Bridge, Pinebank Arch, Gothic Bridge and the Southeast and Southwest Reservoir Bridges.

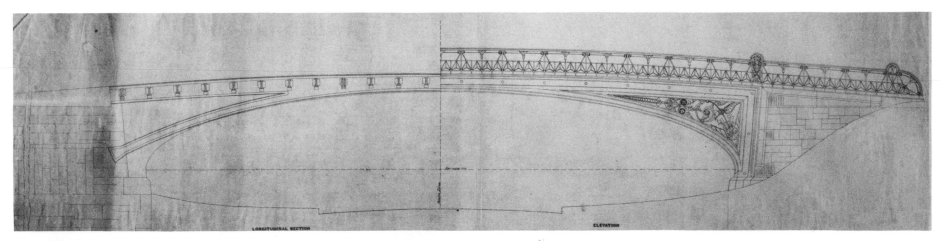

Longitudinal section and elevation. Original working drawing. 1874.
Municipal Archives.

Plaza Lights. Anton Schutz. Aquatint. 1930.

GLOSSARY

Abutment A masonry mass that takes the downward thrust of an arch or a vault.

Ashlar A squared and finished building stone.

Balcony A platform enclosed by a low wall and which extends from the main wall of a building or a bridge.

Balustrade A railing formed by balusters, that is, upright supports in a variety of turned shapes, customarily swelling towards the base.

Belt Course A horizontal course or row of masonry united in one line and extending across a wall.

Blind Arcade An arcade which is made up of two or more arches on imposts or piers, where the customarily open spaces are filled with a wall.

Boss A projecting mass of stone usually carved.

Bunker An enclosed space for storage or shelter.

Bush-hammered Stone with the pitted surface created by a bush hammer, a hammer with one face covered with diamond points, used to pit the surface of stone.

Buttress An abutment or support to strengthen a wall, usually on the exterior.

Cambered "I" Beam A metal beam, with a cross section shaped like the letter "I" given a convex curve.

Cavalcade A procession or a pageant.

Cavaliers Horseback riders.

Cinquefoil Five foils or lobes formed by 5 triangular projections or *cusps*, set in a circle.

Coffer A sunken panel in a ceiling.

Coping A protective top to a wall or a parapet.

Corbelled out Projecting from a wall of masonry (see Balcony Bridge).

Cornice The projecting horizontal upper part of a structure.

Coursing The way in which courses, or layers of masonry, are placed on top of each other.

Crocket Decoration, usually in the form of bunched and curved foliage on the sloping edge of a gable, pinnacle or spire.

Cyclopean rock A huge rock taking its name from the Cyclops, a race of mythical giants with one eye in the middle of the forehead.

Dene A bare sandy tract or low hill by the sea. In Central Park adopted as the name for an open space of ground.

Efflorescence A leaching caused by moisture that leaves deposits of salts on the surface of masonry.

Elevation The height of a structure.

Elliptical arch An arch having the shape of half an ellipse.

Embankment A raised structure to hold back water.

Erosion The wearing away of land or deterioration of masonry.

Foliated ornament Ornament consisting of leafage.

Gneiss A laminated metamorphic rock, the main bedrock of the Bronx.

Gonfalon The flag of a state or one that hangs from a crossbar.

Gothic Revival The architectural style of the Middle Ages which had a revival in this country in the Romantic Era, 1825–1860.

Greywacke A fine-grained conglomerate stone, usually dark grey, quarried on the west side of the Hudson River.

Grotto A cave, given that name when found in an English or Picturesque landscape.

Incisive Cutting into stone as a form of decoration.

Ironmonger A dealer in iron hardware.

Ironwork Decorative work in iron.

Lobe A rounded form alternating with cusps or triangular projections in a circle of tracery.

Loch Scottish for lake.

Megalithic Made of huge stones.

Neo-Classic A revival of Classical architecture from about 1750 to 1850.

Obelisk A four-sided tapering ornament or monument customarily of stone, as Cleopatra's Needle in Central Park.

Ogival An arch that is pointed at the center.

Parapet A low wall on the edge of a roof, balcony, or bridge.

Pier A vertical mass of masonry used for support lacking the shape and detail of a column.

Portal An imposing door.

Puddle wrought-iron A form of pure iron produced by melting pig iron in a furnace, then taken out as a white hot ball with chipping slag and hammered to remove impurities. In genuine puddle wrought-iron, the process is repeated five times to remove all impurities. Not used since 1958.

Quatrefoil A pattern of four lobes and four cusps set in a circle (see cinquefoil).

Random ashlar Ashlar, which is squared, finished building stone, when not laid in a straight line or continuous joints.

Revetment A covering or facing of stone work, usually over a brick or concrete wall, to make it more attractive.

Rockface Stone given a presumably natural surface.

Romantic Era In the United States the era in our literature and in our art that identifies the generation before the Civil War.

Rondel A circular window or opening.

Rusticated voussoir A wedge-shaped block forming part of an arch and given a channeled surface.

Saracenic arch A horseshoe arch, only pointed at the top.

Schist A metamorphic rock in foliated layers, the main bedrock of Manhattan.

Segmental arch An arch formed from part of a half-circle.

Segmental span The same as a segmental arch.

Spandrel The triangular space bounded by the curve of an arch, where the vertical line on the side meets the horizontal line at the top of the arch.

Spring block The block or support on which one end of an arch rests.

Spring line The horizontal line from which an arch begins to curve.

Terminal scroll An ornamental spiral at the top of a column, also a volute as found in an Ionic capital.

Tooled A block of stone whose surface has been given fine shallow vertical grooves.

Trestle A frame consisting of a horizontal member resting on uprights set at an angle and spreading at the bottom.

Tuscan arch An arch whose voussoirs, or wedge-shaped blocks, form a pointed or ogival pattern at the top and a round one at the bottom.

Unitized girders Girders so joined that they form a unit.

Vault, barrel A masonry ceiling, usually semi-cylindrical in shape, which is like an extended arch.

Vault, brick An arched structure made of brick.

Vermiculated A surface of cut stone given indentations resembling worm tracks.

Volute A spiral scroll.

Voussoir A wedge-shaped block found in an arch.

Wing wall Masonry extensions, often serving to support, on a structure.

INDEX

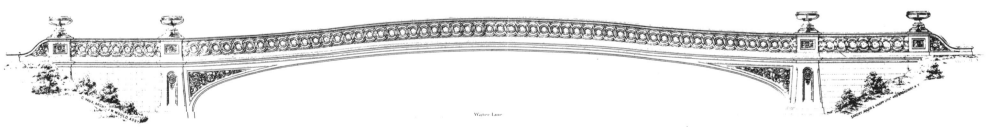

Water Line

BRIDGE FOR FOOTPATH

Bow Bridge.
Third Annual Report, Central Park, for 1859.